TIGERS
BY THE RIVER

A True and Accurate Tale
of the Early Years of Professional Football

Wylie Graham McLallen

x

Mechanicsburg, PA USA

Published by Sunbury Press, Inc.
Mechanicsburg, Pennsylvania

SUNBURY
P R E S S
www.sunburypress.com

For information about special discounts for bulk purchases, please contact Sunbury Press Orders Dept. at (855) 338-8359 or orders@sunburypress.com.

To request one of our authors for speaking engagements or book signings, please contact Sunbury Press Publicity Dept. at publicity@sunburypress.com.

ISBN: 978-1-62006-804-5 (Trade paperback)
ISBN: 978-1-62006-848-9 (Mobipocket)

Library of Congress Control Number: 2017933705

FIRST SUNBURY PRESS EDITION: April 2017

Product of the United States of America
0 1 1 2 3 5 8 13 21 34 55

Set in Bookman Old Style
Designed by Crystal Devine
Cover by Terry Kennedy
Edited by Janice Rhayem

Continue the Enlightenment!

To the memory of my parents,
Ruth and Lyman McLallen

CONTENTS

*A*NTECEDENTS

A S A BOY in Indianapolis, my father owned a thriving business, and all in the family were great fans of the Chicago Bears and the National Football League. The Bears were owned and still coached by George Halas with the color commentator for their games on TV being none other than Red Grange. When they won the championship in 1963, Dad gave me a book about the Hall of Fame, which had just been established, with biographies of the seventeen original inductees, Halas and Grange among them. My father was a kind man who often exaggerated, and when we sat down and talked about this he said that the greatest pro-football team of all time was the Memphis Tigers in 1929. He said they were owned by the man who had invented the modern grocery store and was one of the wealthiest men in the South, and they had on their roster Ken Strong, Mel Hein, Johnny "Blood" McNally, Cal Hubbard, and Ernie Nevers, five of the original Hall of Fame inductees. As a boy he had watched them from the stands of a stadium in Memphis as they beat the Chicago Bears and the Green Bay Packers, and week after week in the fall they played against teams coached by Halas, Curley Lambeau, and Earl "Greasy" Neal with the likes of Red Grange, Turk Edwards, Pepper Martin, George Trafton, Don Hutson, Beattie Feathers, and Bronko Nagurski on the opposing lines and backfields.

Though not disbelieving, I was skeptical of this claim coming out of my father's memory, for it seemed too mythological, and

I had never heard it before; even the rich owner seemed imaginary, for who would invent the grocery store. But Dad was born by the Mississippi River in Memphis, Tennessee, and grew up there and married and started his family there before business and opportunity pulled him and us to the North. And Memphis, appropriately named after the fabled ancient Egyptian capital that was on the Nile, is by its natural setting a place that breeds moods and dreams, and exaggerations, too.

In its long unending flow to the sea, the Mississippi is like time itself as it courses through the heartland of America, engorged by streams and wetlands and other rivers, draining and replenishing and creating and fertilizing in a broad, wet, winding confluence that carries people and ideas and emotions, too. Carrying them all along within itself and on boats and barges and large and small detritus, natural and not, that just appear on its moving surface. Towns and ports have grown on special places along its banks where industry and societies boom. But sometimes, like the long watery shores of great panoramic bends that disappear from its course when the river will suddenly jump banks and switch its path, these towns and industries and ports shrink and almost disappear, too, like the great bends that become horseshoe and quarter-moon lakes left behind in its mighty swath. Time and the river just keep moving along, and, as such, each generation has ideas and accomplishments that are lost in their folds only to be found again when someone decides to go back and take another look.

Often I yearn for the flat fields around Memphis, the intense summer heat, cool relief of the fall, and the sandy banks of the great, ceaselessly surging river. It is these falls and events and cadenced voices some years before my birth that move me to write. The present does not wholly contain the universe; it is but the now part of time's spectrum, a film covering layers of history. Sometimes history, the past, is like a coiled spring; sometimes, however dynamic, it lays all but forgotten, its participants wraithlike shades athletically moving in padded leather gear in the quick dusk of a late-autumn evening.

There truly was once a professional football team called the Memphis Tigers owned by a mercurial genius businessman. And on successive Sundays in December 1929 they actually did play and defeat the reigning National Football League champions, the Green Bay Packers, followed by the Chicago Bears, and, along with the population of the city, without dispute, proclaimed themselves the national champs. When they played the Chicago Bears, and atoned for their only loss of the season, there were three men on the roster—Cal Hubbard, Johnny Blood, and Ken Strong—who would later be among the first players inducted into the pro-football Hall of Fame.

Their owner had even greater ambition for them in 1930. Spurning entry into the NFL, he proposed to build a huge stadium in Memphis so that they could continue to play all their games at home. But it was not to be. The Great Depression broke and deepened, and the brash potent owner lost his fortune; his grand ambitions for a football team a quick and early casualty. Still, they played on for a few more years and played very well. This is the story of their valiant losing struggle against obscurity in the early years of professional football. Though written from a distance of both space and time, the images are still fresh and easily evoked. The past is in the present, and the present is in the past. To go back in time, one need only travel down secondary highways or merely look out the window at an old building.

The streets in Memphis were narrower back then, as Belvedere and other midtown streets remain to this day, and the cars were high, mostly dark colors, and narrower than the ones that came later. Prohibition was the law of the land, making liquor illegal, but bathtub gin was easily obtainable. Bootleggers thrived, but gangsters did not; at least they did not in Memphis, it being a point of pride that the iron hand of "Boss" Crump was tougher than the mob. Memphis had other problems, deeper and more serious manifestations of human complexity that would not really come to the surface for many years. It was two cities within one: that of the white people and that of the black people; and the black people were obscured and stricken with poverty. However, though I felt the admission important, this story is not about the terrible realities of discrimination, innocent by comparison, it is about a vital spirit consumed and an opportunity lost.

It was the time of my grandparents when my own parents were still children (while researching, combing through microfilm of old Memphis newspapers at the Main Library on Peabody and McLean, I came across a picture of my father as a twelve-year-old camper) and, since this is a story about men, a sketch of my two grandfathers can reveal much.

My maternal ancestors, the Grahams, were among the first white settlers in West Tennessee, arriving in Shelby County with a land grant to establish Raleigh just a few years after the founding of Memphis. Their generations moved slowly. My great-grandfather, a son of the early settler, was too old to fight in the Civil War, and granddaddy, nearly a generation older than my grandmother, was past forty when he finally married. He was tall and handsome, thought by many to be the best-looking man in Memphis, and pragmatic and gregarious. Younger members of his large, extended family remember him on a porch uninhibitedly playing the banjo. And so good was his ability to meet and know people that he seemed to know everyone. Once, to see how real this social prowess of his really was, two friends tried to trick him by dropping fictitious names. Granddaddy, now knowing it was a hoax, humbly claimed he knew not of whom they spoke.

He lived with his family on Carr Avenue in East Memphis, an area now known as Midtown, and was not inclined toward church, although many in the family were. Granddaddy distrusted the feverish invitations to spiritual quests, along with the often severe request for financial sacrifice, so ubiquitous in the Southern Church. He made his living as a car salesman, often working at agencies owned by close friends, and was quite a sports fan, traveling with my grandmother to Chicago in 1927 to see the Dempsey-Tunney Fight, that of "The Long Count," and after the fight silently encountering the defeated Jack Dempsey in an elevator of the hotel where they were staying. Had Granddaddy gone to Hodges Field to see the Tigers play, and a few times most likely he did and probably without my grandmother, he would have worn a hat and, as the season progressed into winter, a long coat.

It is for certain that my other grandfather, who was a great fan and had favorites among the players, attended the Tigers' games and always took my father along. On cold days they heated bricks and wrapped them in blankets to take with them to the ballpark. When his youngest brother once arrived from out of town, Grandpa took him to Hodges Field on a Sunday, especially excited to see the big end from Ole Miss, Austin Applewhite. During these years my father's family lived across the street from the grand, all-but-completed, intended home of the team's most prominent owner, Clarence Saunders. As a boy my father remembers watching Lee Saunders, the son who made a noted contribution as a player, turn the corner at Central and Goodwyn driving a Stutz Bearcat and wearing a raccoon coat.

Grandpa went to the old Memphis University School on Manassas across from Forrest Park, the steps to the old building still remain, and skipped his graduation to attend the Indianapolis 500 as a member of the Frenchman Jules Geaux's pit crew. (Geaux won the race, and to celebrate, cracked a bottle of champagne across the hood of his racer.) However, Grandpa was a good student and also a fair athlete, playing well on the football team. After sojourns at Wabash College and the Wharton School of Finance, he alone of all his siblings returned to Memphis and went to work for his uncles at Nickey Brothers Lumber Company. There his enthusiasm and brains created much success; he involved them heavily into the production of veneer, himself a member of the national veneer grading rules committee; and he was made general manager with a salary of over $20,000 a year, a considerable sum in those days. My paternal grandparents first lived on Galloway Avenue near Overton Park, where my father could hear the lions in the zoo roar at night, and then in the late twenties moved to a much larger house on Goodwyn Avenue across the street from Sam Nickey and a few homes down from Will Nickey, the uncles who owned the sawmill.

Then as now, Goodwyn Avenue, running between Central and Southern, was a street of grand homes. When grandpa moved there it was the eastern-most extent of town and, though residence included membership in the Memphis Country Club at its southern end, it was not yet paved and did not yet extend across Central Avenue into Chickasas Gardens because that area, once the grounds of Clarence Saunders's grandly conceived estate-in-progress, was just starting to be developed.

Saunder's "Pink Palace" on Central Avenue

On the southeast corner of Central and Goodwyn lived Mrs. Dan Hamilton, a wealthy woman from New York City, her father a founder of Mutual of New York, who came south with affordable romantic notions to marry a poor but handsome aristocrat from Charleston and build an enormous, and incongruous by design, oriental mansion. Years later when the house went for sale and she was unable to obtain the price she wanted, she had it torn down. When Saunders was building his palace across the street, naturally enough, a conflict developed between these two unusual people. Saunders started it by voicing a negative opinion of the fence around Mrs. Hamilton's property. She replied, having the last word, that she would save him the disturbance by purchasing his new estate from him. As events turned out, had the offer been real, it would have been a very good sale for Mr. Saunders.

βEGINNINGS

NVISIONED BY Early Maxwell, a tall, young native sportswriter then working for the *Memphis Press-Scimitar* (it was he who nearly forty years later would bring the Beatles to Memphis) as a small but potential part of a growing and developing sport, the football team started in the middle of November in 1927 when thirteen men assembled for practice at Hodges Field on the northwest corner of Waldron and Jefferson. Most of them had college experience, a few had been area prep stars. The heaviest man on the squad was a husky medical student who weighed 200 pounds. Edward Solomon, president and general manager of New Brys Department Store, announced that his store would sponsor the team, saying, "they will be the best equipped independent professional football team in the South," and named them the New Brys Hurricane. The first game scheduled was against a semi-pro team from Arkansas.

On the last Friday night of the month Maxwell arranged for the team to go through practice drills during the halftime of a prep game at Hodges Field (7,500 capacity). Red Schneider's punting delighted the packed stands. Then on Sunday afternoon before a much smaller crowd they beat the Beebe Aggies 6-0. Afterwards, two Aggies, half-Indian quarterback Joe Fuqua and end Walter Horn, quit Beebe to join the Hurricane and practiced with them during the week.

On the following Sunday they beat a team of former collegians from Jackson, Tennessee, but coach Gil Reese was dissatisfied

Early Maxwell on the radio

with their play, claiming Fuqua did not have enough protection to get off his passes, and their next opponent was a seasoned club, the St. Louis Blues, that had reportedly won their last ten games and boasted of having two big NFL veterans on their line.

New uniforms arrived, and the jerseys were grass green. Tickets sold for a dollar, but it rained and less than 1,000 people showed up. The field turned to mud as the teams struggled to a scoreless tie. Both sides agreed to a rematch on Christmas Day, and the Hurricane bolstered its squad with collegians who had finished their season. Dave McArthur and Charlie Rice came from the Tennessee Vols, and Slick Vincent from Alabama, as Fuqua and Horn went back to Beebe. The Blues returned on Christmas Eve and spent the night at the Claridge Hotel. Again, less than 1,000 people attended the game, but the Hurricane

TWO OBSTACLES IN HURRICANE'S PATH

Roy Tandy, Center   Zev Carman, Tackle

St. Louis Blues comin' to town

scored early on a pass from Futrell to Reese and played tough defense; Schneider intercepting four passes, and McArthur breaking through the line several times to nail opposing runners for loss of yardage; and the Memphis team won 7-0.

There was talk about a New Year's day game against a team from Arkansas that boasted of having the great Indian Joe Guyon in its backfield, but it was never scheduled. There were no more games for the year, and the season ended with the Christmas victory over the Blues. The Hurricane disbanded, several players traveling down to Jackson, Mississippi, to play in a benefit game against a squad of Mississippians. (With Goat Hale at halfback, the Mississippi team won 31–0.) Though the team had gone undefeated in its inaugural season, it was hardly an auspicious beginning for a professional sport in a teeming, resilient American city with a past that yearned for its own kind of glory.

In the late 1920s, Memphis, a preeminent Southern city with strong ties to the past, had a population of 250,000 and was already making headway as a distribution center. Though not much older than one hundred years, it had been a long hundred years steeped in change. Founded on the Chickasas Riverbluffs as a real estate venture by three Nashvillians, one of whom was Andrew Jackson, it began as a bawdy river town, from which sprang the political likes of frontiersman Davey Crockett, and grew in stature as the most important port of the Mississippi River between Cairo and New Orleans. Early in the Civil war, in June of 1862, it fell to the North, defeated by Union gunboats in a brief battle on the river, and, though a detachment of Confederate Cavalry commanded by General Nathan Bedford Forrest made a sudden and frightening foray into the city in 1864, remained subdued through the rest of the war. It was in one of the large mansions along Beale Street where Grant began his initial planning of the Vicksburg Campaign.

The post-war years saw the residency of Jefferson Davis and tens of thousands of newly freed Negroes flock to the city from the fields of Alabama and Mississippi and the heavy river traffic and marketing of cotton. On the cobblestoned stretch of dock, now used for parking, that slants down to the Wolfe River where it merges into the Mississippi, cotton bales and dark, sweat-glistening Negroes crowded next to huge paddle wheelers lined up along the bank. Then in the summer of 1878 yellow-fever arrived, carried upriver by the mosquitoes, and decimated the population. The city lost its charter and became a taxing district. But it rebounded from this disaster through the patient labor of loyal citizens.

Besides being on the great river, there were other natural blessings: huge underground reservoirs of pure filtered water, a surrounding region covered with hardwood forests, and the flat, open fields of fertile delta land planted in long, straight rows of cotton. With the Mississippi as a conduit, Memphis became a city of global commerce. The ringing buzz of a saw became a common sound as large tracts of outlying timber were cut and cleared and sawmills sprang up, at one time over 200 within the city limits, shipping lumber by rail and river barge to cross continents and oceans. And on Front Street cotton bales moved in and out of the wide entrances to the tall, narrow, brick buildings lining the row where the brokers organized business and rang their profits. Memphis was the center of the hardwood lumber industry, and a huge cotton market, selling and trading more cotton than anywhere else in the world. In the last decades of the nineteenth century, the city grew and prospered in a disorderly manner; blotted with mule markets that spread for

Commerce on the River Front

acres, its first skyscraper, the ten-story D. T. Porter Building, arose on Main Street in 1890.

There were murders every night on Beale Street where itinerate Negro peddlers flocked with harps and fiddles and harmonicas and moving feet. They made soulful tunes of their harsh, sad lives on this bright and lively dark venue, which had degenerated from the pre-war mansions of the rich into squalid gambling dens and bars, where the multitudes of their brown, bronze, and black brethren crowded and frantically sought entertainment among the con men and prostitutes and criminals who worked the street nightly. And yet beauty arose from the fertile stench of this roiling turmoil, for it was here that a gifted, black musician named W. C. Handy, playing the piano and trumpet in the brassy juke joints, put to paper and wrote the first songs of that kind that came to be known as "The Blues." As the sun set across the great river not far from Beale Street, the white folks listened to the strident, tinkling blues of W. C. Handy, too, but within the clean confines of luxurious hotels and private ballrooms.

Hardly out of touch with its heritage of an unruly river town, a tall, redheaded man named Edward Hull Crump arrived one day from Holly Springs, Mississippi, and walked along Front Street fascinated by all the activity. Crump, industrious and intelligent, spurred on by the poverty of post-war years, married into wealth, though not before establishing his own worth in business, and entered politics. By 1910 he had in his grasp the reins of political power throughout Shelby County and became for the next forty years "Boss" Crump, a benevolent political dictator. He gave focus and direction to city politics, managed to clean up (or at least contain) vices that had always plagued the city, and provided for a pattern of steady growth.

Memphis became endowed with doctors and merchants and expanded its boundaries. But downtown where the people worked, gathered, and shopped, remained the hub of activity. There were men's clubs and hostelries. Court Square was alive with pedestrians. The Exchange Building was built, followed by the white, towering Sterick Building. Seen from across the river in Arkansas, the skyline took on prominence.

War erupted in Europe, and when the United States entered in 1917, Memphis lost its share of sons on the battlefields. One local surgeon, Dr. Frank Smythe, organized a hospital ship and crossed the Atlantic Ocean to France where, under the auspices of the US Army, the equipment and staff were incorporated into a hospital in Neuilly, and in 1918, with Dr. Smythe as post commander, the French government decreed the hospital "an institution of public benefit" in recognition of services rendered during the First World War and authorized it to receive bequests and donations as the American Hospital in Paris: thus, even a noted Parisian institution has roots in Memphis. When the war ended, there was a disregarded prohibition and keen fascinations and many possibilities unexplored as new technologies were introduced. But always there was the hard, earthy struggle, so well-known in the South, to survive and advance.

This was the first great era of professional sports. When Jack Dempsey fought the Frenchman Georges Carpenter at Madison Square Gardens in 1923, the gate brought in over a million dollars. Bobby Jones won golf's Grand Slam and then promptly retired from professional tournaments. Tennis was dominated, and the game elevated, by the gifted Bill Tilden. Remarkable feats were also achieved in auto racing as the Indy winners approached and then exceeded average speeds of 100 m.p.h. over the course of the race. And each summer professional baseball took hold of the national conscious; in 1927 New York Yankee teammates Babe Ruth and Lou Gehrig surged toward astounding batting numbers, Ruth finishing the season with sixty home runs and Gehrig not far behind with fifty-four; and some of its finest players came from the South. All these exploits were closely followed through newspapers, movie news-reels, and over the radio. Though there were some very strong yearnings, the South was not then a major participant. How-ever, there was plenty of minor league action. Memphis had the Chicks, managed by Tommy Prothro (father of the famous foot-ball coach of the same name), who played at Russwood Park.

The predominant spectator sport in the South was College Football. Vanderbilt fielded great teams (so frustrated was the University of Tennessee that a young assistant coach at West Point named Robert Neyland was hired with the edict BEAT VANDERBILT, and this he proceeded to do as football fortunes shifted irrevocably to the eastern end of the state) and there was Alabama and Georgia, Georgia Tech, The University of the South at Sewanee, LSU, and, even further south down in New Orleans, Tulane. These schools would play on Saturday afternoons before 20,000 and 30,000 people. But in the North there had been a growing and developing movement toward professional football.

One story has pro football beginning in Latrobe, Pennsyl-vania, in 1895 when a YMCA team, about to play a club from neighboring Jeannette, asked sixteen-year-old high school star John Brallier to fill in for their injured quarterback. Brallier declined until an offer of $10 induced him to play. Latrobe de-feated Jeannette and started a trend: other teams began paying for good players.

Professional football, given birth, soon shifted its ground of battle to the Midwest where public enthusiasm was more re-sponsive, especially among blue-collar workers. In Ohio, after the turn of the century, a fierce rivalry sprang up between the Canton Bulldogs and the Massillon Tigers.

Pro football was brutal in these early years, unorganized, and had an unsavory reputation. Most of the players worked in factories and mills during the day. Paid collegians played under assumed names to avoid association. Some teams were disbanded a week after being formed and scheduled games were often canceled. In World War I it all but ceased to exist. But in 1915 there was a portent of the future: The Canton Bulldogs hired Jim Thorpe for $250 a game, and to watch him debut against Massillon, 8,000 people showed up, a huge crowd in those days for an obscure sporting event.

After the war a corn starch manufacturer in Decatur, Illinois, named A. E. Staley hired twenty-five-year-old George Halas to organize a company football team; businesses often advertised themselves this way. While trying to line up competition, Halas heard about plans to organize a league, and on September 17, 1920, got together with a few other men in the showroom of an automobile agency in Canton, Ohio, that was owned by Ralph Hay, who also owned the Canton Bulldogs; and along the fenders and on the running boards of the new cars, there was beer there to tickle their minds, the National Football League, although it would not take that name for another two years, came into being. The future did not look very bright, but they were tough men, and a savior was not long in coming.

In the mid twenties, like a great comet streaking across the sky, Red Grange captured the national spotlight. At the University of Illinois his dazzling ability to run with the football made him one of the most famous men in America, earning him immortality as "The Gallopin' Ghost of Illinois." In 1924 Michigan was ranked the best football team in the country, but when they played Illinois late in the season, Grange broke loose for four touchdowns in the first quarter, every time he touched the ball, scored another by game's end, and rushed for 400 yards as Illinois crushed Michigan 39-14. "All Grange can do is run!" Fielding Yost, the Michigan coach, had spitefully remarked before the game. "And all Gallicursi can do is sing!" came the Illini post-game retort.

In the early twenties, if the weather was fair, in the big cities of the North 10,000 people might appear at the ballpark to watch a professional football game. Unlike the collegians, who attracted multitudes to huge stadiums on fall Saturdays, the pros were often publicly defamed, and teams existed hand-to-mouth. Then in late November of 1925, with only a few games left in the season, in a room at the Morrison Hotel in Chicago, Halas signed Grange to play for the Chicago Bears. Thanksgiving came cold and wet and still 36,000 fans showed up at Wrigley Field to watch Grange's professional debut. The Bears and crosstown

The Gallopin' Ghost

rival Chicago Cardinals played to a scoreless tie, but large profits at the gate convinced Halas to extend the Bears' season.

They barnstormed the country. In Philadelphia a crowd of 35,000 sat through driving rain as Grange scored two touchdowns to lead the Bears to a 14-7 victory over the Frankfort Yellowjackets. The next day in New York City, it was early December now, people climbed fences and crushed the gates of the Polo Grounds as 73,000 watched Grange and the Bears beat the Giants 19-3. A few days later in Boston against the Providence Steamrollers (Jim Crowley and Don Miller, half of the famed Four Horsemen of Notre Dame, played in the Steamrollers' backfield) 25,000 saw the Bears lose 6-9. Hard times were still ahead, and the unsavory reputation would linger yet longer, but professional football had made its first permanent stitch in the American fabric.

Paternal Interest

*F*ATE CLICKED IN Memphis in the fall of 1928. The papers announced that the city could look forward to a full season of pro football. Phil White returned to coach and captain the team. White (6' 2", 210 pounds) had been an all-American halfback at Oklahoma in 1920, and after attending medical school in Memphis, played three years of professional football with the New York Giants. The first game was scheduled for October 14 against an auto dealer's club from Nashville. The Memphis team still had several medical students and former prep stars on the roster, but its character and name was about to change. A prominent businessman had stepped into the picture because his son wanted to play pro football. The new name of the team was the Sole Owner Tigers.

The team lost their first game this year to the smaller and quicker O'Geny Greenies, who had Gil Reese in their backfield and several players that had been members of a famous prep team at Montgomery Bell Academy. By the end of the month Lee Saunders, the son of the new owner, had joined the squad, and on the first weekend of November they traveled to Cairo, Illinois, with eighteen players to play the Cairo Independents. White and Lee Saunders made the trip in a small, private plane while the rest took the train.

Phil White would play for Memphis just this one full season, and this before much money was infused and public attention focused upon the team, but he was probably the best player the Tigers would ever have at quarterback. Against Cairo, he

Some of Stars In Lineups of Game Today at Hodges

CAPT. PHIL "ZERO" WHITE H.B. MEMPHIS

GIL REESE H.B. NASHVILLE

CAPT. CHIN JOHNSON Q.B. NASHVILLE

SOLLY COHEN F.B. MEMPHIS

WEST TENN. TEACHERS DEFEAT DELTA ELEVEN | How Sole Owner Tigers and Genys Will Stack Up In Contest at Hodges Today | PINE BLUFF ZEBRAS AT LAST DETHRONE

The start of a season

completed seventeen of twenty-one passes; Ernie Marquette caught thirteen, one for a touchdown, and delighted the sparse crowd with quick, agile moves. The Tigers made eleven first downs to Cairo's four, but one of the Independents intercepted a pass and ran seventy yards for a touchdown. The game ended in a 7-7 tie.

Back home they practiced at the fairgrounds, working on an aerial attack, and on the following Sunday played a team from Dyersburg called the West Tennessee Collegians. White led the Tigers to a 16-6 victory (prior to the game the Central High varsity scrimmaged against an alumni squad), but afterwards was very critical of his offense, whose sloppy play caused a pass interception. The Collegians disbanded when their offer for a rematch was rejected. Tiny Knee, their small Indian halfback, joined the Tigers, and some of their other players went to the

Tigers' next opponent, the Arkansas Panthers. The Panthers were a bigger, faster team than the Collegians, which is why they were scheduled instead, and outweighed the Tigers ten pounds to a player. But on the next Sunday, after failing to connect in the first quarter, White's passes found their mark, and the Tigers scored almost at will, blasting the Panthers 33-0.

Then Maxwell brought in a team from an Oklahoma Indian reservation called the Hominey Indians who had played against NFL teams and had not been beaten in two years. In the early years of professional football, there were many Indian players who came from reservations, and through the years the Hominey Indians would be the Tigers' best rival. Maxwell offered them twice the cash guarantee of any yet paid to a visiting team. In an effort to promote the game, when the Indians arrived on Saturday they donned head feathers and other tribal regalia and paraded the streets near downtown.

With over 2,000 people in the stands at Hodges Field, the Indians, much bigger and more experienced, beat the Tigers 7-0 in a brutal game. One of the medical students, Otho Alfred,

200-Pound Tackles of Indians Who Meet Sole Owners "11" Here Sunday

BUCK HARDING   ALVRO CASEY

Indians in town

Local Gridders Who Oppose Indians Sunday

Bottom row—Left to right: Bob Cook (Sewanee) right end, Norman Thornton (Southwestern), center and tackle, Byron Futrell (Arkansas) halfback, Lee Saunders (Sewanee) halfback, Tiny Knee (Wabash) fullback, Frank Trelawney (Southwestern) fullback and end. Middle row—Left to right: Frank Payne (U. T. Doctors) tackle, Ernelle "Red" Cavette (C. B. C.) left end, Joe Pickering (Southwestern) left guard, and Doc Price (Southwestern) halfback. Top row—Left to right: Phil White (U. T. Doctors) coach, captain and halfback, Newman Jones (Central High) right guard, Charlie Atkins (Central High) guard, and Otho Alford (U. T. Doctors) left tackle, Ernie Marquette (C. B. C.) quarterback, and Shorty Neil (U. T. Doctors), not in photo.

The 1928 Tigers

broke his ankle and had to be helped off the field. Several other players were also injured. Still, the Tigers were able to move the ball through the air, and the teams agreed to a rematch on December 16. In fact, the Indians offered to remain in town and play again on the following Sunday. But Maxwell thought his team too battered for such a strong opponent so soon and instead scheduled another car dealer's club from Nashville, the Bachelor Motor Eleven, and added Duke Kimbrough and a half-back named Johnny Leake to the roster.

Playing for the Nashville team were Gil Reese, who like many players of the era went from team to team during the season, former Tennessee Vol fullback Dick Dotson, and the great Vanderbilt all-American end Lynn Bomar. Tickets sold for $1.00, and a fair crowd showed up. Bomar was out of shape and did not play well, and the Tigers, though they were not expected to win, established the start of a proud tradition of winning football. They scored on a blocked punt, and then on a touchdown pass from White to Marquette, and beat the favored Nashville team 13-0. They won again on the following week, beating the Cairo Independents before less than 1,000 fans. White passed well, and Tiny Knee, crouching and darting down the field, rushed for long yardage. The final score was 13-0.

Then came the return of the Hominey Indians, and on Saturday morning, the day before the game, the Tigers were pictured in *The Commercial Appeal*: fourteen men in football uniforms without much padding. The Indians had added a 260-pound tackle named Tiny Roeback to their roster and stayed at the Gayosa Hotel. Tickets sold for $1.50 with the winner to get 60 percent of the gate. But it rained that Sunday, and the game was played in a sea of mud before another small crowd. The Tigers lost 13-20, but the game was not close. The Indians used their weight advantage and bottled up White for most of the afternoon.

One of Indian Giants Who Will Face the Tigers This Afternoon

TINY ROEBUCK (L. T.), 260 Pounds.

Indian Tiny Roebuck

The team disbanded after the game, its players dispersed, some of them to pick up more money in all-star games. The next year their owner would devote to them more time and attention. And one interesting fact: Lee Saunders, taken on because of his father's money, had proved himself worthy, if not very talented, on the field.

Clarence Saunders and His Juggernaut

C LARENCE SAUNDERS was born on a tobacco farm in Virginia in 1881. Hard times of the post-Civil War had fallen upon the South. His mother died when he was four, and the family moved to Palmyra, Tennessee, a village close to the Kentucky border near Clarksville. At fourteen, impatient with formal education, he quit school to work in a general store sixteen hours a day for $4 a month with room and board. After three years, desiring to see more of the world, he moved to Birmingham, Alabama, and worked in the coke oven of a steel mill as a night-shift supervisor; but he returned to Tennessee and the grocery business. In 1900, making the rounds among rural merchants in a horse and buggy as a traveling salesman for a wholesale grocery firm in Clarksville, he saw many small stores fail and concluded that they used too much of their profit margins to pay the clerks and took heavy losses on credit sales.

He married in 1903 at the home of his bride in McLeansboro, Illinois, and moved to Memphis to take a sales job for the wholesale grocers, Shanks-Phillips & Company. Then, with a partner in 1915, he organized the Saunders-Blackburn Company that sold its goods for cash and encouraged its customers to do likewise. Soon, in the form of the self-service grocery store, came a dramatic and brilliant turn in his career. It was an idea he had used earlier in some of the stores he had sponsored. "I

Interior of an early Piggly-Wiggly store

tore out the counters, put in aisles and turnstiles and decided to let the customers wait on themselves." Overhead expenses were cut to a minimum, and the interior was designed to lead people through the entire stock before they left.

Mysterious billboards began to appear around Memphis, on which the only words were "Piggly-Wiggly." After nearly a month the words were "Piggly-Wiggly is coming." Later there were more words without apparent meaning, such as, "Mrs. Brown told Mr. Brown to stop by Piggly-Wiggly on his way home." Then came the announcement that Piggly-Wiggly would appear downtown at 79 Jefferson Avenue on September 11, 1916.

There was a brass band at the opening and roses for all red-haired women. Shoppers had the experience of being able to pick over groceries. And on its first day of business, operating on a cash-only basis, the first Piggly-Wiggly took in over $400, an enormous amount for a small retail store of the time. And while this may not have been the first self-service grocery store, the few other attempts were not so efficient and people-friendly, nor were they accompanied by the promotional genius of Clarence Saunders, so this time the idea spread. Revolutionizing a basic part of life, Clarence Saunders gave the world the modern grocery store. By 1922 there were 1,241 Piggly-Wiggly stores across the United States and Canada, half of them owned by Saunder's firm, Piggly-Wiggly, Inc. And to further the growth of his company, Saunders had it listed on the New York Stock Exchange.

Mr. Saunders was an ebullient man who liked people and had an elfin face with brown hair turning gray. Always well dressed in public, he was of average height and rather stocky build. His grandiosity, coupled with enormous energy, made him atypical and sometimes seemed to impair his judgement. But it also created much fun and improved the quality of life for millions of people. In 1922, at a time when his wealth may have exceeded $10,000,000, he started building a palatial estate on Central Avenue, employing for a year about 100 people on the construction.

Stonemasons from Scotland laid the pink Georgia marble. The building was surrounded by 160 acres with a lake, an eighteen-hole golf course, a trapshooting field, and was said to have had its own power plant and pumping and heating system. Saunders named it CLA-LE-CLARE for his three children, Clay, Lee, and Claire, and had spent nearly a million dollars when news came there was trouble on Wall Street. A group of brokers had lowered the price of Piggly-Wiggly stock by short selling the shares. Saunders hired George Livermore, a prominent Memphis broker, and quickly went into action. It was rumored that a small, black valise he had traveling with him on the train to New York City contained $1,000,000 in cash.

By March 19, 1923, the stock had risen from $39 to $77, and Mr. Saunders had control of nearly all 200,000 shares. But the next day he discarded Livermore's advice and demanded delivery on the stock. The price jumped to $124 a share. The Wall Street Exchange declared that a corner existed, removed the firm from the trading list, and gave the short-sellers five days, instead of the usual twenty-four hours, to honor contracts. The price dropped drastically, and Saunders returned home broke.

It is probable that Saunders had bought stock by putting up stock he already owned as security for loans from banks in New York, St. Louis, and Washington, and that during the suspension of trading trapped bears had prevailed upon bankers to call his loans, forcing Saunders to sell his shares and providing the stock with which trading was resumed, to meet their demands. Saunders later said that some of his friends had become uneasy and took their profits too soon. By August the new owners of

Piggly-Wiggly, Inc. had forced him out of the business, and his pink palace was eventually given to the city.

Back in Memphis he moved his family to a hotel and rode street cars to the federal court. A week after the bankruptcy hearing was over he borrowed $12,000 from friends and, giving it the name "Clarence Saunders," started another self-service grocery store. But his former firm, claiming that even the use of his name was the property of Piggly-Wiggly, Inc., filed a lawsuit. Saunders fought the injunction that tried to prevent him from opening another store and in a dramatic courtroom appeal declared that he was "the sole owner of my name." He won the case, and the new store was called "Clarence Saunders, Sole Owner of My Name."

Mr. Saunders could be irascible. In 1926 he engaged in a fistfight, for which he publicly apologized, with John Burch, the secretary and advertising manager of Piggly-Wiggly, Inc. About a month after this altercation he was indicted, and then acquitted, for a mail fraud charge stemming from his attempt to corner the market. And all along the size of his second grocery chain kept increasing. Eastern bankers began to invest heavily in Clarence Saunders Stores, Inc., and by 1928 there were 153 Sole Owner Stores across the nation.

Clarence Saunders was again very wealthy and built a 300-

Clarence Saunders

acre estate called Woodlands east of town on Park Avenue. (It is now the Lichterman nature Center.) On the grounds were a huge log cabin mansion, a fifteen-acre lake, an eighteen-hole golf course, and two tennis courts. That summer he entered politics by supporting Governor Henry Horton in his bid for reelection, aligning himself against E. H. Crump, who was backing McAlister. During the campaign, using full-page ads in the paper, Saunders and Crump publicly denigrated each other. (McAlister swept the vote in Shelby County, but Horton carried the state).

Then in October, on the eve of their silver wedding anniversary, Carolyn Saunders sued him for divorce charging "outburst of temper tirades and abusive language." And at the same time their second son was casting about for a career in professional football. Lee Saunders had played collegiately in the backfield of the University of the South at Sewanee and wanted to play for the local professionals. So his father conferred with Early Maxwell and assumed financial backing of the team. But other than providing a place for his son on the roster and giving them a new name, his involvement with the team for the rest of the year was limited to just paying their bills. However, in 1929 he threw himself into this new acquisition, and the results were spectacular. Mr. Saunders was one of the first and most radical of the great egotistical sports team entrepreneurs.

That fall the character of the team changed almost immediately. When the Tigers held their first practice of the year, September 15 at Hodges Field, tryouts were open to the public. Some of the men were area prep stars, and others had played at Southwestern College in Memphis, but Saunders had hired a full-time manager, Alfred Goldschild, who was arranging for the signing of more talented players. Gone were Phil White, regrettably so, and Otho Alfred and the rest of the husky medical students. Soon big men with impressive football credentials began arriving from out of town and replaced the local players on the practice field. But one local player who remained and in the years to come would be one of the team's best players was Cliff Norvell, a former all-Memphis tackle at Humes High.

By the time they played their first game, Saunders had assembled some of the finest young players in the country and would search out more throughout the season. At halfback there was Bucky Moore (5' 11", 185 pounds) who was called "The Dixie Flyer." So celebrated had he been in New Orleans, where the year before at Loyola he had surpassed Red Grange's single season record by rushing for 1,580 yards, that a nickel candy bar was named after him; it, too, was called "The Dixie Flyer." He joined the squad on Tuesday, September 23, along with a fullback from Sewanee named George Mahoney.

The Fightin' Tigers

Then came a flurry of linemen; the best being Larry Bettencourt (6', 205 pounds) from California. Twice selected all-American as a center at St. Mary's, a small Catholic school then as prominent in football as Notre Dame, Bettencourt was one of the most heralded collegians of the twenties. There was also Joe Davidson, a 215-pound tackle formerly with the Chicago Cardinals, Tommy Thompson, Memphians Fred Getz and Red Cavette, and the return of Duke Kimbrough.

Hugh Magevney, the Central High coach, was hired to coach the Tigers. He had played under Knute Rockne at Notre Dame and would employ some of his mentor's variations of the single-wing formation, virtually the only football formation then in use.

In the single-wing the halfback was positioned just outside the end like a wingback, hence the name single-wing, seven men were on the line, and the ball was snapped directly to the quarterback or the fullback. It was an effective ball-control offense, outnumbering the defense at the point of attack and offering deception when the players were bunched and able to go in different directions. On defense the Tigers played a diamond-seven: seven men on the line with the backs positioned in a diamond.

On the Sunday morning of the season's first game, September 29, Mr. Saunders placed a full-page ad in *The Commercial Appeal* boldly announcing, "These Tigers of mine will fight till there's not a bit of fur left. If you like good football – the best football – clean football – fighting football, we've got it for you right here in Memphis. We've gone to a lot of trouble and expense to give Memphis a real football squad and we are out to win a national championship." His intent declared, all that was left to be done was support from the fans. And though out-of-town talent had taken over the roster, Memphian Red Cavette was named team captain. It was also announced that a special section on the west end of the stadium would be reserved for Negroes with the admission price the same: 75¢ for adults, and 25¢ for children twelve and under.

Bucky Moore and Dick Hitt, a halfback from Mississippi College, were pictured in the sports pages: Moore had intense eyes and a scrape on the bridge of his nose; Hitt was ruggedly handsome. The weather was dry, the day hot and dusty, and 2,000 fans heeded Mr. Saunders's exhortations and went to Hodges Field in the afternoon to watch the Tigers play a team from Buckner, Illinois.

Mahoney started things rolling in the first quarter with a line smash into the end zone, then Hitt scored twice, and Lee Saunders, quarterbacking the team in the second quarter, scored on a twenty-five-yard run. The heat began to take its toll of fatigue, but the Tigers had good reserve strength, and in the second half Bucky Moore broke loose, scoring touchdowns on runs of forty-five and fifty-six yards in the third quarter, and in the fourth quarter reversing his field to go seventy-five yards for another. The Buckner team, though they had Big Ten players on their roster, were not very good. Just as the game ended,

Make Debut on Saunders Tigers Today

Dick Hitt (Halfback).   Bucky Moore (Halfback).

Hitt and Moore

Cavette caught a touchdown pass from Hitt to make the final score 52-0.

Mr. Saunders had had his first proprietary taste of competitive glory and liked it so much that a few days later he signed a contract paying $1,000 rental fees for each game played at Hodges Field, later to be reduced to 10 percent of the gate, and provided an additional $100 on each player for uniforms and equipment. He also made efforts to upgrade the schedule, no longer would the Tigers play teams averaging 165 pounds a player, and for the next opponent replaced a semi-pro team from New Orleans with the Kansas City Independents, who had on their roster a famous all-American end from Michigan named Harrigan.

On the following Saturday afternoon the Tigers held a long signal drill and practiced punting and passing on the field behind Central High (Crump Stadium had not yet been built there), and more players joined the squad; a fullback named Louis Gremillion from Loyola, and Memphians John McCarroll and Dode Farnsworth. Still, the roster was not complete, and on Sunday morning Mr. Saunders told Tiger officials "to go out and get the best team possible and spare no expense." Attendance

Two Stars and Backer of the Saunders Independent Tigers

Red Cavette (L. E.), Captain.　　Clarence Saunders and Mascot.　　Larry Bettencourt (Center).

Clarence Saunders with Lynx Mascot

did increase that afternoon, and in the midst of all the roaring in the stands, roaming along the sidelines carefully tethered, was a live wildcat from Arkansas.

The game started badly for the Tigers, but they turned it around. In the first quarter Mahoney was knocked out and carried off the field, and later in the period a Kansas City player intercepted a pass and returned it eighty yards down the sidelines for a touchdown. But then the defense started to dominate with Farnsworth's punts, putting Kansas City deep in their own territory, and the offense sustaining long drives by plunging Hitt and Gremillion through the line. Before the end of the first half Tiny Knee went off left guard into the end zone, and Memphis took the lead. Then in the fourth quarter they exploded for twenty-seven points in what was described in the next morning's paper as "a knockout blow to a worn and tottering fighter." It started with Bucky Moore catching a punt on his own twenty-yard line and in a spectacular run zigzagging all the way back down the field, then minutes later Hitt scored on a sixty-yard run. The final score was 38-6. At the end of the game three Kansas City players were taken across the street to the Baptist Hospital to be treated for minor wounds.

The next week they went on the road, the only time all season, to play the O'Geny Greenies in Nashville. During the week, practicing under the arc lights at Hodges Field, Magevney rotated two backfields. When they left on Saturday Saunders had built quite an entourage: twenty-six players, three managers, three trainers, the coach, and the owner took the train to Nashville, followed by about 150 fans in autos and buses, and spent the night at the Hermitage Hotel. On Sunday Bettencourt watched from the sidelines with a bruised knee as Frank Liddon took his place at center.

Hitt crashed across the goal line for the only score in the first half; an O'Geny drive had earlier been halted by Farnsworth's interception. In the second half the Tigers dominated and wore their opponents down. Norvell blocked a punt, and Getz recovered it in the end zone. Then, once again, Bucky Moore broke loose, scoring twice on long runs to put the game out of reach. In the final minutes, Hitt intercepted a desperation pass and raced fifty yards to the end zone. The Tigers had beaten a good Nashville team by a score of 33-0 and on Monday night, back in Memphis, they were guests of honor at the Orpheum Theatre.

Now trying to achieve national recognition, Saunders scheduled the Cleveland Panthers. The Panthers, whom Maxwell had ambitiously and unsuccessfully tried to schedule in 1927, were a relic from the pre-war years when pro football was centered in Ohio. In fact, in 1916, their first season, they had beaten Jim Thorpe and the Canton Bulldogs. Another notable victory had come more recently, in 1926, when as part of Cash 'n' Carry Pyle's short-lived American Football League, they beat Red Grange's New York Yankees. Over the years they had accumulated an imposing record of 140 wins, 7 ties, and 13 losses, and they had in their lineup some very big players. Their center, Al Derhammer, was 6' 2", 225 pounds, and their left guard, Tiny Potter, was 6' 8" and 210 pounds. Lured by the largest guarantee ever offered from a southern club, the Panthers rode the train south, stopping in St. Louis on Friday, and arrived in Memphis on Saturday, October 19, spending the night at the Chisca Hotel on Main Street, which was a few blocks north of Grand Central Station.

During the week the Shelby County Athletic Commission officially endorsed the Tigers. The team practiced at Mr. Saunders's vast estate on Park Avenue. More seats were added to

In Lineups of the Panthers and Tigers Here Today

KNEE
H. SAUNDERS
TIGERS

KERR
L.T.
CLEVELAND
PANTHERS

SADLER
H.B. CLEVELAND PANTHERS

CAPT. CAUETTE, L.E. SAUNDERS TIGERS

Panther Lineup

Hodges Field, bringing its capacity to 10,000, and the Junior League, directed by Mrs. Neeley Mallory, helped sell tickets to the upcoming game.

Much was written in the papers about Larry Bettencourt. So far he had been outstanding. He had long legs and a barrel chest, stopped opposing runners before they got started, and opened wide holes for the offensive line. The game against Cleveland was seen as a chance for him to really prove himself.

Five thousand people were in the stands on Sunday afternoon, the largest crowd yet, but hardly comparable to the 20,000 in Knoxville the day before to see Tennessee play Alabama. The Tigers scored on a pass from Hitt to Thompson in the first quarter, and the defense stopped Cleveland cold. Norvell scored a safety in the second quarter. And in the second half, with the opponents tired and winded, the offense exploded. Moore broke loose for four touchdowns, running behind Gremillion's interference, scoring three in the last eight minutes of the game on runs of eighty, sixty, and forty-five yards. Tommy Thompson kicked five extra points, and the final score was 43-0.

Players and fans were jubilant. A crucial victory had convincingly been won. That night at Grand Central Station, a huge stone monument-like building facing north on Calhoun between Second and Third streets, the team threw a surprise party for Mr. Saunders as he boarded a train to New York City leaving on a business trip. He was accompanied by his son Lee, who would be back in town for next Sunday's game against the St. Louis Trojans.

The Tigers were confident and hungry for even greater victories, and, though concerns expressed about the next opponent would prove needless, John McCarroll, who had played with and against many of the Trojans as a collegian in St. Louis, said that Bettencourt would at last be pitted against a very good player named Lee Sheib, who had made some all-American teams at Washington University. During the week some changes were made to the lineup. Kimbrough temporarily departed to Greenwood, Mississippi, his position at right tackle filled by Chris Arnoult, and Getz and Marquette limped around doubtful if they could play on Sunday. As the team went through a short signal drill on Saturday afternoon, practicing without their leather helmets, a wire came from Mr. Saunders telling them not to let up. They took the field on Sunday, though the crowd was smaller than the week before, with the fervor of a mighty rebel army, displaying their brassy strengths, and massacred the Trojans by a whopping 67-0.

Bucky Moore, whose high school coach, Goat Hale, was in the stands, and three other backs scored two touchdowns each (this brought Moore's season total to thirteen touchdowns) as Bettencourt dominated the center of the line on both offense and defense. The Trojans failed to even cross midfield as the Tigers continued to score even when they sent in the reserves. Tiny Knee came off the bench and ran for a touchdown, and Cavette scored on a pass from Hitt.

Saunders had created a juggernaut. Though no profit has yet been realized (and would not be, but, then, this was symptomatic throughout professional football), it seemed that the owners magical touch in revolutionizing the grocery business might also apply to his sporting venture. He had high ambitions for his football team and some stunning ideas that he would soon reveal to the public. But the fulfillment of genius was to elude him here, and his influence would not last, for already the

Trojans Next

winds of change were in the air, and they would overpower and permanently subdue him.

On the previous Thursday the stock market had made its first awful lurch. Over the weekend President Hoover said, "The fundamental business of the nation is on a sound and prosperous basis." But on October 19, infamous Black Tuesday, the price of stocks plunged drastically, and the nation was on the threshold of The Great Depression. Along with practically every other tangible aspect of life, it would have a disastrous effect upon the future of pro football in Memphis. Clarence Saunders was a brilliant man, but also just like everyone else: a human being whose earthly fate is mostly determined by powerful forces external to the mind and body.

Black Tuesday had struck; the future looked foreboding; already there was fear. But in the sports pages of the *Memphis*

Red Grange, Galloping Ghost Will Gallop Here on Nov. 23

Red Grange will gallop in Memphis

Press-Scimitar the Tigers continued to be much heralded. Naylor Stone wrote, "Clarence Saunders' Tigers are plenty good. They've been riding high, wide and ferocious over good and bad opposition. We'll know just how good they are after Nov. 23. On that date the local independent club will line up against Red Grange, Illini's old gallopin' ghost, and the Chicago Bears."

It would be the first time for the Bears to play in the South. Saunders gave them a bigger guarantee than the one he had given the Cleveland Panthers and also paid $2,000 to the city's two Catholic high schools to postpone their annual game scheduled at Hodges Field on the same date. With the Bears to play in three weeks, their next opponent was the Hominey Indians and public enthusiasm was at its peak.

When the Indians came to town, perhaps because Mr. Saunders had been so generous with the Bears, they wanted a bigger guarantee. The matter was settled on Saturday in Mr. Saunders's office at 461 South Front Street, and his blood was up. With officials of both teams present, he phoned George Halas in Chicago and made the request that a team be sent down to play the Tigers the very next day. Halas agreed, but there was no need to go any further because the Indians suddenly became tractable and accepted the terms offered. But Saunders was not finished with them yet.

On Sunday, November 3, despite recent rain, the stadium was filled to capacity; 10,000 people, the largest crowd to ever see the Tigers play. When the game started the owner was not present: he was outside watching the last of the crowd trying to filter into the stands. The Indians fumbled the kickoff, the Tigers recovered and were about to score when Mr. Saunders made his entrance. Play was stopped and officials down on the field were told to restart the game so that Mr. Saunders and those who were late could see it from start to finish. There was some disagreement, the officials protested, but the owner had his way, and so, for perhaps the only time in history that such an arbitrary condition was ever imposed by an owner upon a professional football game, the Indians received the kickoff once more. This time they mounted a short drive and

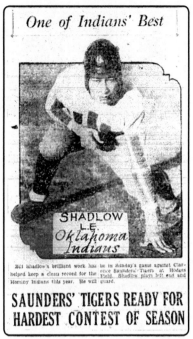

One of Indians' Best

SHADLOW
L.E.
Oklahoma
Indians

Bill Shadlow's brilliant work has be in Sunday's game against Clarence Saunders' Tigers at Hodges helped keep a clean record for the Field. Shadlow plays left end and Hominy Indians this year. He will guard.

SAUNDERS' TIGERS READY FOR HARDEST CONTEST OF SEASON

Indian threat

punted. The soggy field and huge Indian line made it hard for the Tigers to advance, so they punted it back to the Indians. Then disaster struck for the visiting team: throwing one of the few passes of the day, Hitt intercepted and dashed 30 yards to the end zone. The Tigers scored again in the second quarter to lead 13-0 at the half.

But the Indians were a stronger opponent than any they had yet played, and it was close in the second half. Late in the fourth quarter the Indians got a break deep in Tigers' territory when Getz lost his temper and threw a punch. The ball was moved half the distance to the goal line, and though victory was out of reach, the Indians made the touchdown and the extra point for a final score of 13-7.

The Tigers did not play on the following week, and more players were added to the roster. Austin Applewhite (6' 2", 210 pounds) and Tiny Drouilhet, a 220-pound tackle who was a college teammate of Bucky Moore, joined on Thursday. Then on the next Wednesday, November 13, Saunders made headlines in the *Memphis Press-Scimitar* with the announcement of plans

Complete Wire Reports of UNITED PRESS, the Greatest World-Wide News Service

Memphis Press-Scimitar

FINAL

6TH YEAR—NO. 282   14 PAGES   MEMPHIS, TENN., WEDNESDAY, NOVEMBER 16, 1929.   PRICE 3 CENT

SAUNDERS PLANS HUGE GRID STADIUM

A New Stadium?

to build a 60,000-seat stadium in Memphis. He reasoned that a big stadium would lower the price of a ticket and still yield him greater profit; basically the same volume principle he had successfully applied to the grocery business. Because of the large guarantee given to the Bears, tickets to the game would cost $2.00, and for the team to just break even, Hodges Field would have to be filled to capacity.

The game with the Chicago Bears meant a lot to Saunders by giving his team more credibility and promise to their future. When a rumor began spreading that Red Grange was not going to play, he wired Chicago to insist that the Bears show in full strength or not at all and that Grange must play at least twenty-five minutes. Halas sent a wire back to Saunders the next day emphatically stating that Grange and the entire Bear squad were coming to Memphis intent upon victory. Then another rumor began to spread, and this one was reported in the paper: Mr. Saunders wanted his Tigers in the NFL.

They remained undefeated through the next weekend, playing the Bonneycastle club from Louisville. Saunders spent Saturday in Knoxville among 30,000 people at Shield-Watkins Stadium watching Tennessee play Vanderbilt, casting covetous eyes on the great Vol back Gene McEver. Bonneycastle arrived in Memphis with a following of about 100 fans and spent the night at the Peabody Hotel. The opponents were bold and confident, and their managers predicted they would thwart the Tigers' attack. Several Tigers, interviewed over the radio, were asked about these remarks and replied that they were prepared to play their best.

A large crowd was anticipated. Against the Indians it had been very congested. Seven ticket booths were set up, and police were there to direct traffic. But it rained and only 1,500 people attended as the teams struggled in the mud. Bonneycastle punted

SAUNDERS AFTER BERTH IN NATIONAL PRO LEAGUE

Doug Wycoff and Ivan Williams, Former Tech Stars, and Other Football Greats May Enlist With Local Eleven in 1930

NFL Future

whenever they got the ball. The Tigers moved down the field but were always stopped short of the goal line. Then with six minutes remaining, Cavette caught a short pass from Hitt and with mud flinging off his cleats dashed into the end zone for a 7-0 victory.

The next day at Luke Tinsley's cigar stand, located in the Cotton Exchange Building on the corner of Front and Main Streets, tickets went on sale for the Bear game. Crowded sidewalks downtown were abuzz with the name Red Grange, and there was much talk about the impending confrontation between Bettencourt and the Bears' center George Trafton. Trafton (6' 1", 230 pounds), though now immortalized in the Hall of Fame, was a mean and difficult player, whom Halas once had to kick off the team.

The Chicago Bears of 1929 were a team ready for transition. Key players such as Paddy Driscoll, Link Lyman, Joey Sternaman, and Trafton were getting too old, and there was a growing rift between the two owners, Sternaman and Halas; Halas having retired as a player the year before. "We had two offenses," a player later recalled, "one devised by Halas, the other by Sternaman. Nobody knew what to expect on any play. People were running into each other on the field." This would be settled the next year when Halas made his first retirement as coach. The two men would put aside their contentions and hire Ralph Jones, an early proponent of the then not-yet-very-well-developed T-Formation, from Lake Forest College to coach the team.

Yet, despite present internal discord, the Bears had gotten off to a good start and at the end of six games had won four, tied one, and lost one. Then they collapsed and lost eight of the next ten. When they first came to Memphis they had a record of 4-5-1 and a passing game still intact. Walt Homer, a former

Bonneycastle

all-American triple-threat back at Northwestern, ran the team on the field. The ends were Luke Johnsos and Garland Grange, the younger brother of Red.

Saunders spent the first part of the week attending the National Fox Hunt Championships in Nashville and would anxiously phone Magevney about the offense attack. Bill Meriwhether from Hendrix College was added to the roster to improve the kicking game, which had not been very good against Bonneycastle, and tickets to the game, to be played on Saturday, sold so well that by the end of the week people were trying to scalp them. It was at this time that Memphis reaped one of the benefits of a vigorously promoted, high-profile sporting venture and played host to a distinguished visitor.

Red Grange came to town ahead of his teammates, arriving by train on Thursday morning. He was taken to Woodlands to play nine holes of golf on Mr. Saunders's private course and in the afternoon attended a prep game at Hodges Field between Catholic High and Memphis University School. MUS won the game, and afterward, Grange had praise for Henry Krouse, the MUS captain, and Sturla Canale of Catholic High. Then in the evening he was guest of honor at the Annual Gridiron Dinner of the Newspapermen's Club at the Peabody Hotel where, seated near the middle of a long table in the front of a large banquet hall, many people were introduced and charmed by the great man's sensible and generous personality.

Walt Holmer

It was Grange's first visit to Memphis, and the media was impressed. The *Memphis Press-Scimitar* printed a picture of him shaking hands with a small boy at the banquet and, along with Mr. Saunders, he was heard over The Salesman Sam and Art Hayes Show broadcast live by WMC from Lowe's Palace on Friday afternoon.

Though Memphis was thrilled with Grange's presence, the weather was not cooperating. An early snowstorm began to fall; by noon on Friday there was five inches on the ground. At Hodges Field thirty men worked through the night, scrapping snow, burning the turf dry with gasoline, and placing down a cover of straw by the early light of dawn. Grange's teammates arrived that morning at Union Station. The straw was removed, and when the gates opened at noon on Saturday, 7,000 people filed through the turnstiles.

The Tigers were up for the game, but in the first quarter it was Red Grange who made the first score by dashing fourteen yards to the end zone. Bucky Moore answered with a fifty-five-yard touchdown run. Bettencourt was playing well, and the Tigers

Red Grange and One of His
Staunchest Local Admirers

Red Grange

stayed even until the fourth quarter when Holmer began to find holes in their pass defense. In rapid succession he threw for three touchdowns, and the Tigers were defeated 19-39 for their only loss of the season. The Bears boarded a train and returned to Chicago, where the next day they were beaten 7-19 by the Buffalo Bisons.

Maxwell was working hard in the background and, with the aid of Mr. Saunders, arranged an impressive schedule for the remainder of the season. The next game, scheduled on December 1, was a rematch against the Hominey Indians, a week later came the Notre Dame All Stars, then the last two games, a crowning end to the season, would be against the Green Bay Packers and the Chicago Bears. The roster was strengthened by adding Norman "Red" Strater from St. Mary's and a 260-pound tackle from LSU named Jim "Fat" Wilson.

The rematch against the Indians was a game made harder by a deluge of rain that cut attendance to less than 1,500. The field was muddy, and by halftime it was so dark the lights were turned on. The Tigers had done most of their scoring by then; Moore threw for two touchdowns in the second quarter and just about had the game won. But in the third quarter Whitey Shelton, the only Caucasian on Hominey's roster, broke loose on a thirty-yard run and scored for the Indians. The Tigers came back in the fourth quarter. Farnsworth booted a punt out of bounds at the Indian one. The ensuing punt was blocked, and the Tigers scored a safety to win 16-7. Afterwards, they added Shelton and Tiny Roebuck to their roster.

But they were losing money, and overtures came from New Orleans to finish the season down there. Saunders, however,

The First Bear Game

had no intention of moving his team from Memphis and made it clear they would remain in town. Some of the triumphant gloss of the first half of the season may have been tarnished by the loss to the Bears, and by the close scores of recent games plagued by bad weather. And though the venture had thus far lost the owner $15,000, it was to him still only a small amount, and he remained undaunted. Often things do continue on continuing, and Saunders definitely had a way of keeping the party up.

Tigers vs Notre Dame All Stars

Much of the public glitter that may have been lost was quickly replaced when the Notre Dame All Stars, assembling for the first time all year with thirteen former Irish all-Americans among them, began their prestigious arrival. Lead by Texan Christy Flanagan, not all of them had played at Notre Dame; Ed Healy was a Dartmouth Alumni whom Halas was later to call "the most versatile tackle of all time."

But again the weather went against them, turning cold and wet, and a crew worked Saturday night into the early morning hours of Sunday to prepare Hodges Field. Keeping the field dry, gasoline burned in orange undulations and cast an eerie light on the dark surrounding streets, as Mr. Saunders himself appeared once to watch the workmen's progress. The game began

In Lineup of Tigers and Notre Dame Stars Here Today

1—Jack Chevigny, halfback, Notre Dame Stars. 2—Bucky Moore, halfback, Saunders Tigers. 3—Gene Hardwick, half-back, Saunders Tigers. 4—Elmer Wynne, fullback, Notre Dame Star. 5—Christy Flanagan, fullback and captain, Notre Dame Stars. 6—John McMullen, tackle, Notre Dame Stars. 7—John Illis, guard, Saunders Tigers. 8—Doug Wycoff, fullback, Saunders Tigers.

Tiger & Irish Stars

under gray, threatening skies with the stands half full. The All Stars came out onto the field wearing green jerseys and gave the Tigers a full game, actually outplaying them.

The Tigers scored first when in the first quarter Doug Wycoff plunged into the end zone. But the Irish tied it up in the second quarter on a pass to Flanagan. Then the game became a punting duel until the fourth quarter when Bucky Moore at last broke loose and returned a punt deep into Irish territory. A few plays later he dashed into the end zone to give the Tigers a hard-fought 12-6 victory.

It was at this time that Saunders began to stack his roster with NFL veterans. Wycoff, a bruising 220 pound fullback from the Statin Island Stapletons, told the owner about a teammate named Ken Strong who, he said, was the best player in the NFL. Strong was a threat to score whenever he had the ball; as a collegian at NYU the previous year, he had lead the nation in scoring with 161 points, and he could punt almost the length of a football field. Saunders quickly sent a wire to New York offering Strong $350 a game. Lineman Jess Tinsley (6', 205 pounds) and

New Star of Saunders' Tigers | *Strong's Running Mate*

Strong and Wycoff

Jake Williams (6', 205 pounds) were acquired from the Chicago Cardinals, and from the Bears came tackle Joe Kopcha (6', 225 pounds). Saunders also added Christy Flanagan, hired boxer Shifty Logan as special team trainer, and increased practice to twice a day.

The Green Bay Packers, undefeated champions of the NFL, arrived on the following Saturday with twenty-one players and spent the night at the Tennessee Hotel on Union Avenue. During these years after the official NFL season was over, its teams would roam the country as far away as the west coast to make extra money playing games well into the month of January. The Packers had finished the season undefeated with twelve wins, beating their archrival Chicago Bears thrice, and one tie. During the previous summer coach Curley Lambeau, a haberdasher in the off-season, had strengthened their roster by acquiring Mike Michalske, Carl Hubbard, and Johnny "Blood" McNally. The Packers had been a good team before with Red Dunn at tailback, Verne Lewellyn at halfback, and Lavie Dilwig at end, but with the new additions they played with a bone-crushing defense and a wide-open offense. Michalske (6', 210 pounds) and Hubbard (6' 5", 265 pounds) lead an aggressive line that snuffed out opposition, and Johnny Blood, whom Lambeau paid $110 a week with the stipulation that he not drink liquor

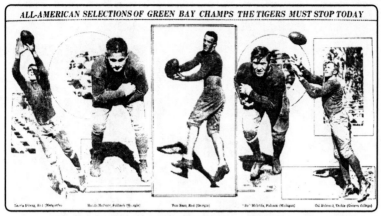

ALL-AMERICAN SELECTIONS OF GREEN BAY CHAMPS THE TIGERS MUST STOP TODAY

Packer Stars

after Wednesdays, was the fastest man in the league, a great defensive back, and one of the best pass receivers then playing football. After their last victory, the one that brought them the championship, 20,000 people awaited their arrival in sub-freezing temperatures at the train station, dancing and carousing all night to welcome them back to Green Bay.

In Memphis, however, Saunders had tilted the scales. The Tigers' starting lineup averaged 209 pounds, the line averaging 218 pounds. The Packers' starting lineup averaged 207 pounds, their line also averaging 218 pounds. So the odds had about been evened, and the strategy planned by the home staff was in part the reason that the first half of the season had been such a resounding success: the big men would play in the first half and wear down the Packers, Bucky Moore would not even start, and then in the second half the smaller, more agile players would be inserted. Dick Hitt was injured, so Strater started at quarterback.

On Sunday, December 15, the weather was clear and balmy, fine for late autumn football, and the stands at Hodges Field were almost completely full. The game was broadcast back to Green Bay; the spectators were noisy and active. The Tigers drove down to the Green Bay 4-yard line, but the Packers held. Urged on by the crowd, the Tigers were playing inspired football, especially on defense, with Strong swapping punts with Johnny Blood and Lewellyn, and the Packers were unable to get their aerial attack going. There was no scoring in the first half.

Saunders and Some of His Hopes to Stop Green Bay Champs

Left to right: Larry Bettencourt, center; Joe Kopcha, guard; Clarence Saunders, owner of Saunders' Tigers; Norman Snead, quarterback; Kenneth Strong, fullback; Doug Wyckoff, halfback.

Saunders and Players

In the second half the Tigers broke loose. Strater threw a fifty-yard touchdown pass to Austin Applewhite in the third quarter. The point after attempt was blocked, but a few minutes later they recovered a fumble at the Packer thirty-five-yard line where Strater threw a short pass to Moore and the Dixie Flyer ran into the end zone. This time the dropkicked point after was good and the game almost turned into a rout. Trailing 0-13 in the fourth quarter and deep in their own territory, the Packers attempted a lateral. Dunn tossed the ball toward the sidelines to Lewelleyn, but Drouihet stepped between them to intercept and ran fourteen yards to the end zone. The score was now 20-0, but the Packers avoided a shutout. With less than two minutes to play, it was dark and the arc lights were on, they recovered a fumbled punt near the Tigers' goal line and punched the ball across in three rushing plays.

The game had been brutal, and there were several injuries. Tinsley was taken to the hospital for stitches to a wound suffered when somebody kicked him in the back of his head. And though there were grumbles from the Packers about the result ("the boys seemed to be off their form and out of condition," Lambeau told reporters) the Tigers had convincingly prevailed, and the next morning a front-page headline in *The Commercial Appeal* proudly proclaimed, "Saunders Puts City on Pro Football Map." A

Factors in Saunders Tigers Scoring Against Green Bay Champs

Top—Kenneth Strong Getting off one of his sensational punts   Below, Left to R
Whitey Shelton, Doug Wyckoff and Austin Applewhite.

Packers Game

SAUNDERS PUTS CITY ON PRO FOOTBALL MAP

Tigers Reach Pinnacle by Beating Green Bay Champs.

LAY CLAIM TO TITLE

Team Built Up in Two Months, Smears Undefeated Record of Team of 11 Years' Reputation. Large Crowd Attended.

Headline

few hours later a similar headline in the *Memphis Press-Scimitar* read, "Tigers Put City on Football Map." But whoever the cause for its success, the city was truly proud and jubilant, and there was more to come. The next week saw a rematch with the Chicago Bears, and from the Packers, Johnny Blood, Carl Hubbard, and 250-pound tackle William Kerne were added to the Tigers' roster.

Snow fell heavily across the middle of the country. There was a blizzard in Chicago, and in Memphis the Tigers canceled Wednesday's practice. On Thursday Mr. Saunders and several of his players were guests at a Junior Chamber of Commerce luncheon held in the Claridge Hotel, and in the afternoon the entire squad practiced long and hard and confidently. Then, on Friday, Red Grange returned to town. Somewhat of a familiar face now, during the day he spoke before various high school assemblies and in the evening had dinner in the home of George Canale on South Belvedere. Already there was a crew at Hodges Field scraping off snow and clearing the seats in the stands.

Trio of Chicago Stars Who Meet Tigers Here Sunday

Bill Senn (Halfback)   Walter Holmer (Fullback)   George Trafton (Center)

Bear Star and Great Runners

In *The Commercial Appeal* on Saturday a two-page ad was placed by several local businessmen and boldly headed, "Clarence Saunders Tigers – World Champions! Thanks! Thanks!" Displaying individual pictures of several players, it urged fans to attend the last game of the season. "The Tigers have worked and fought to show you that a great football team could be put together at Memphis and for Memphis." It read, "We surely want you to be on hand tomorrow at Hodges Field with the largest crowd of the season so that by such a record the Tigers will be certain that you want them back for more football next year." General admission to the game was $1.50, reserved seats were $2.50, and box seats cost $3.00; the same prices as the Green Bay game.

Red Grange and Mr. Saunders, along with Tigers Bettencourt, Wycoff, and Ken Strong, were again heard over The Salesman Sam and Art Hayes Show in the afternoon. The rest of the Bears arrived that night at Grand Central Station on South Main. On Sunday December 22 it was cloudy and cold, so cold that many fans stayed at home and the stands were only half full. Small warming fires burned around the field at halftime.

The Tigers drew first blood late in the first quarter when Strong kicked a thirty-five-yard field goal. The Bears quickly came back on a sudden strike through the air when Holmer

Game Action

found Garland Grange standing at the goal line. But in the second quarter Moore caught a short pass from Strater and dashed fifty yards down the sidelines for a touchdown to give the Tigers the lead for good. Victory was sealed in the second half when Applewhite caught a pass off his shoestrings and rushed deep into Bear territory to set up a plunge by Wycoff to make the score 16-6. The defense kept the Bears pinned down deep in their own end of the field only to spend the rest of the afternoon punting out of trouble. When the game ended, the Tigers were avenged and had nailed their pennant high on the mast of pro football.

"As a result of their victory the Saunders Tigers can justly file claim to the supremacy of professional football of the land," wrote *The Commercial Appeal*. But it was bittersweet for Mr. Saunders. His son Lee had broken his leg near the end of the first half and was carried off the field in a stretcher to a waiting ambulance.

Most of the players returned home for the holidays. Bettencourt, John Illia, and Getz drove to California in Bettencourt's new auto. Maxwell tried unsuccessfully to interest Saunders in professional basketball, nor did Mr. Saunders attend an annual meeting of the National Football League in Dayton, Ohio, in January of the New Year. He wanted the Tigers to play all their games in Memphis and on the strength of their performance in the season just past, along with the size of the new stadium he had planned, figured he would be able to schedule any NFL team he desired. But Clarence Saunders would not own the Tigers in 1930. Caught in the crunch of the Depression, he was financially overextended, and his grocery empire had begun to founder.

Fall From Grace

BANKRUPTCY WAS FILED against Saunders in July 1930, and his company lost control of 150 stores. He blamed eastern bankers who had made large investments in his company, calling them "Wall Street stock manipulators," and the Depression for his failure. However, he insisted he would stay in professional football, and from his office at South Front sent representatives to notify A. P. Hunt, the general manager of Hodges Field, that all dates scheduled for his football team would be retained. He said that he would go ahead and build the big stadium he had said he would build, and that players such as Ken Strong, Christy Flanagan, Whitey Shelton, Larry Bettencourt, and Austin Applewhite would still play for him. But these were only proud, defiant words from a defeated man. In fact, his estate on Park Avenue was up for sale, and he was planning to move to California. By the end of August, Mr. Saunders was out of professional football, and all his players were released from their contracts.

But the Tigers had too much wind in their sails to be ignored, much to the accomplishment of their bankrupt former owner, and a group of businessmen wanted to keep them going. So they would be further sustained, carried along by their own volition, guts, a little glory, and a few bright men who perhaps saw that the future would not be wasted on professional football. This was the time, the early thirties, when the beast that was pro football thrashed violently through a wilderness and not only refused to die, but to even retard; in the opaqueness,

Maxwell in a meeting with executives

actually honing itself into something better. The Tigers were not at the center, but nor did they go unnoticed. At the end of this season the men who managed them failed to take advantage of an opportunity that, which although then may have seemed inauspicious, could have made them part of history.

By 1930 Memphis was the thirty-seventh largest city in the nation and, though the sport was unprofitable, the Tigers were one of the cheapest ways to advertise the town. The *Memphis Press-Scimitar* wrote that they "gave Memphis splendid national publicity as the town of the national football champions." So on an evening in early September several prominent businessmen, ready to carry on where Saunders had left off, met in a suite at the Peabody Hotel and established the Memphis Professional Football Association. Six men worked out the details. Their goal was for sixty men each to invest altogether $4,250. Almost immediately thirty-four men came forward, officers were elected, and an office was set up in the Randolph Building. One of the first things done after securing the use of Hodges Field was to hire Early Maxwell as manager and director of publicity and send him to the big cities of the Midwest to scout for players and schedule games.

The first practice of the season was held at Hodges Field on September 26, and it appeared that the team might even be stronger than the year before. Most of the members from last year's squad were back; Bettencourt, who had spent the

Some Stars of Saunders' Tigers Who Are Back This Season

Retuning Tigers

summer in Texas playing minor league baseball (and hitting thirty home runs), was named the coach. Applewhite returned after his brief career as a heavyweight boxer had come to an abrupt end in Greenwood, Mississippi, earlier in the month: after breezing through six overmatched opponents, he was knocked out in the third round of a fight refereed by none other than Jack Dempsey. And Bucky Moore was also back, though he had not planned on it. He had returned to his college alma mater as an assistant coach, but after watching a few scrimmages, the crash of pads, and the exhilaration of fast, deft movement, his mood changed, he wanted to play, and he returned to Memphis.

Bettencourt was given a salary of $225 a week, one of the highest in the country. But when the Tigers signed Billy Banker, they paid him even more: $265 a week. Banker, an all-American halfback at Tulane in 1929, had matinee idol looks. In fact, his contract released him from weekday practices so that he could appear in the movies. And along with John Illia, who had apparently been signed in the first place only to keep Bettencourt company, two more linemen from St. Mary's, George Ackerman and Hoot Herrin, were added to the roster along with a fullback from Ole Miss named Cowboy Woodruff. The first week of practice was closed to the public, only stockholders could attend, because it was rumored that the Hominey Indians had sent someone around to spy on the players.

Mr. Saunders donated all the old uniforms, equipment, and practice apparatuses. In appreciation, Sunday October 5 was declared "Clarence Saunders Day" at Hodges Field. He was in California, but his daughter Amy Claire would be there to represent him. Tickets went on sale at Otto Schwill's Drugs on South Main. The Indians arrived at Union Station on Friday night (Billy Banker was arriving a few blocks east at Grand Central at just about the same time) and did not practice on Saturday. Loudspeakers were being installed at the stadium so that, along with play-by-play of the game, the highlights of the World Series could be broadcast to the crowd. The Indians had apparently neglected to train and practice at all, because they were overweight and out of shape, and the Tigers pounced on them.

Soon after the kickoff, Whitey Shelton returned a punt, fumbled at the goal line, and Getz recovered in the end zone. Then the Indians attempted a pass, Banker intercepted and ran thirty-four yards for a touchdown. A few minutes later Ackerman scored on a run. The Tigers led 21-0 at the end of the first quarter, Bettencourt sent in the reserves, and still they rolled on. Moore made a spectacular sixty-yard scoring run in the second quarter. At halftime a marching band performed down on the field. And in the third quarter, which opened on a long Tiger drive ending with Banker bucking into the end zone, Moore scored again on pass reception. The Indians mustered hardly any offense, and the final score was 43-0, an auspicious start to the new season.

They kept up the tempo by trouncing the Kansas City Cowboys (the same team they had beaten the year before when

Coach of Indians

Chief Buck Harding

they were called the Independents) 40-7 on the following Saturday under the arc lights at Hodges Field in what may have been the first nighttime pro football game played in the South. Dominating the line of scrimmage, Moore was allowed to break loose for long yardage, once zigzagging the field to score from fifty-two yards out. But Applewhite had a bad night, he kept dropping passes, afterwards claiming that Banker threw the ball too hard, and attendance was down. However, overall, things looked pretty good, and the next day columnist George Bugby wrote in the *Memphis Press-Scimitar* that the "Memphis Tigers loom as a stronger team than the one that took the grid for this city at the start of last season's spectacular march to the Nation's honors."

Bugby had a colorful style and provided analysis, focusing on the ability of Billy Banker, even giving him a moniker:

SEVERAL SPOTS MUST be bolstered, however, to give the Tigers the strength they boasted at the latter part of the 1929 season . . . For instance, something will have to be done about providing at least a semblance of interference for Billy Banker . . . He was accorded about as much help in his cutbacks off tackle Saturday as if he were holding a lone position in the backfield . . . It appears not yet what Banker could do if he could get the type of interference he gives when others are carrying the ball. On several of Bucky Moore's touchdown dashes around the ends Banker was the unsung hero of the occasion. In one instance he took two potential tacklers out of Bucky's way to give the 'Dixie Flyer' an open field for the goal.

Local grid fans want to see the Tulane flash star . . . His great passing, punting, and corkscrew jaunts thru the line have been the feature of Tiger games to date . . . All in all, the "Blonde Blizzard" stacks up as the greatest player who has cavorted on a local field since Ken Strong's flying cleats spurned the Hodges Field grid in the Tigers' Triumphs over Chicago Bears and Green Bay Packers. In some respects Strong excels Banker. The erstwhile Violet Flash probably is a better punter, tho not greatly so, and may be slightly more dextrous in hurling passes . . . on the other hand, Banker probably is the greatest ground gainer, and undoubtedly excels on the defensive. His vicious tackling has been a revelation to local grid followers.

All-Americans With Local Tigers Against Indians Today

Tiger All-Americans

And he attributed the relatively thin crowd, about 2,500 people, to "the fact that Saturday night is not an auspicious time to hold a game, or that the local fans did not figure the Cowboys strong enough to give the Tigers much of a battle . . . At any rate the team deserves better support when it faces the Portsmouth Spartans here Sunday."

From Ohio, the Portsmouth Spartans of the NFL were the biggest team in pro football and were loaded with talent. Their line, averaging 219 pounds from end to end, was anchored by Dick Brown, a 220-pound former all-American center at Iowa. Their backfield was even bigger than their line. Father Lumpkin, a 220-pound former Georgia Tech all-American, was the quarterback; the fullback was a 240-pound Indian from Oklahoma named Mayes McLain. Lumpkin was used primarily as a blocker in an offense geared for the run. They had another all-American at halfback, the fast, shifty Willie Glasgow from Iowa, who was a noted broken field runner. Given a $4,000 guarantee, they came to Memphis with a 3-1-1 record.

The Tigers practiced hard. Bettencourt told a reporter, "If we can beat the Spartans then we're ready for any outfit in the nation." He knew that the game would be won in the trenches and added bigger men to the starting line. Norvell was replaced at left tackle by 220-pound Roy Blackledge, and Applewhite, who had been taken out of the starting lineup because of his poor play against Kansas City, was reinserted at left end. And because of the size of Portsmouth's line, they worked on an

In Spartans' Lineup Against Tigers at Hodges Today

Willis Glawgow (hb)   Mayes McLain (fb)   ' Father'' Lumpkin (qb)

Spartan Stars

aerial attack. On Sunday October 19 Bettencourt played his best game as a Tiger, blocking and tackling all over the field and intercepting passes.

The day was warm, and under blue skies well over 5,000 people attended. The Tigers moved down the field using a diversified attack of end runs and passes and near the end of the first quarter scored on a pass from Mahoney to Moore. Portsmouth then fumbled at their own 5-yard line, the ball rolled into the end zone, and Bettencourt pounced on it. Ackerman kicked the extra point, the ball spinning end to end through the middle of the goal posts, to give the Tigers a 13-0 lead at halftime. The Spartans managed to ground out yardage with Lumpkin and McLain hitting the line for short gains, and in the third quarter McLain smashed into the end zone. But the Tigers scored again when McLain fumbled deep in Spartan territory and Drouilhet recovered to set up another Tiger touchdown to make the final score 20-6.

Afterwards, the Spartans protested the officiating, but the real difference had been in the strength of the Tigers' line. The battle had been brutal: Mahoney was knocked out, and one of the Spartans had been carried off the field in a stretcher. But while Portsmouth had substituted often, the Tigers did little substituting; eight men in their lineup playing the entire game.

Share in Victory of Local Tigers Over Portsmouth Pros

Whitey Shelton.   Larry Bettencourt.   Fred Getz.   Bear Alliday.

Victorious Tigers

The prestige of the Tigers was now even higher than at the end of 1929; their tenacity was admired throughout professional football. The Portsmouth Spartans were a very good team, and they had been soundly beaten in a convincing manner. Even New Orleans took pride in the Tigers, its newspapers giving space to the exploits of hometown collegiate heroes Billy Banker and the erstwhile Dixie Flyer. Then things began to unravel.

They lost their next game to a team they should have beaten, and the problem was the coach. Bettencourt had let the team peak against Portsmouth and thereafter, although plodded along by a confused management (excepting Maxwell), lost focus. His preparation for the Milwaukee Nitehawks was disastrous. The Tigers had two of the best running backs in the nation, but when the players returned to practice on Wednesday, the offense had been revamped to de-emphasize the running game in favor of long passes. Bettencourt also played favorites. When Butch Simas, another player from St. Mary's, joined the roster that week, arriving on Saturday, he was immediately inserted into the starting lineup as quarterback.

The Milwaukee Nitehawks, an independent pro team, came to Memphis with three losses, but two of those had been recent and close defeats to the New York Giants and the Chicago Bears. On Sunday afternoon Bettencourt was sick and did not enter the game until the second quarter, just after Milwaukee's Ben Franklin had intercepted a pass and raced fifty-three yards for a touchdown.

Ironton Tackles Who Face Tigers Sunday

Left to right—Harold Jesson (University of Iowa), Dick Ambrose (Michigan), Harold Rolph (St. Xavier), Tom Edwards (Michigan), and Ted Hastings (Carthage).

Ironton Line

The Tigers played good defense, but on offense the line, which had been primarily responsible for victory the week before, hardly seemed to function. They gained much yardage on runs by Banker and Moore; though neither broke loose for a long one and long timely punts by Milwaukee's Al Bloodgood kept placing the Tigers deep in their own territory. (Naylor Stone reported, "I've never seen as much fumbling in a single game as was done by the Tigers.") Then in the fourth quarter Bloodgood sealed the victory for Milwaukee by intercepting a pass thrown by Banker and returning it sixty yards to set up a drop-kicked field goal that made the final score 0-9.

It was the first time in almost two years that the Tigers had been shutout, and the loss hurt. However, the game had been well attended, and a rematch was scheduled in three weeks. They added to the roster a big, tough fullback named Tony Holm, obtained by default, and played better the next week against a good team with a great coach. Holm had been an all-American at Alabama the year before and had gone north to play in the NFL for the Providence Steamrollers, where he suffered an injury to his ankle. Upon recovering, he decided to return to the South, and the Tigers signed him for $125 a week.

Some of Tiger Hopes Against Ironton Pros

Tigers Pros

From Ohio, the Ironton Tanks arrived Saturday night and stayed at the Gayoso Hotel. They were coached by Earl "Greasy" Neal, now enshrined in the Hall of Fame for the championship years he had as coach of the Philadelphia Eagles in the late forties. Bettencourt had spent the day autographing pictures of himself at the huge new Sears store on Crosstown. The weather was fair on Sunday, and for three quarters, the team played to a standoff. Then in the waning minutes the Tigers mounted a drive and scored on a pass from Banker to Simas to win 7-0.

There was no game on the following week, a suitable opponent could not be found, so the players held light workouts, rested, and were entertained along with their stockholders as guests of the Lumbermen's Club at a luncheon in the Gayoso Hotel. However, management was busy. Monk Godman, the team's corporate vice-president (and the owner of a downtown pool hall where it was alleged he booked bets on sports events), proposed a charity game in Chicago in December against the U.S. Naval Academy, (the idea was rejected by a high-ranking admiral) and Maxwell was sent to Chicago to negotiate for more football games against competitive opponents.

Maxwell left Grand Central Station on Friday morning and arrived in Chicago that evening. He met with Ernie Nevers and signed a contract for the Tigers to play in Chicago later in the month with a $2,500 guarantee. Then he traveled on to

Nitehawk Players

Milwaukee and negotiated a 60-40 percent split of the gate for the game with the Nitehawks the next week, the winner to get the majority. And when he returned to Memphis on the following Monday morning, he was also able to report to the officers of the corporation that several teams, specifically mentioning the Brooklyn Dodgers, were interested in late-season games against the Tigers.

Autumn rains began to fall, and practice again became earnest. Banker took off from school to prepare with the team, and Gil Reese, after a three-year absence, rejoined the Tigers as backfield coach; a move made by the management probably to restore probity to team leadership and direction on the field, because Godman's confidence in Bettencourt may have already started to waver. Despite the rain, they worked several hours a day on the Christian Brothers College campus using a dummy to practice blocking and tackling. General admission to the game on Sunday was $1.50. By kickoff the rain had stopped and 4,500 people were in the stands.

The Nitehawks were again a tough opponent, but this time the Tigers prevailed. Bloodgood's punts went far, but Banker's went further. The Tigers were outrushed, but Tony Holm gained 100 yards on the ground, and it was an even battle on a muddy field. When either team crossed midfield, the other's defense would rally. The Tigers came through in the second quarter when Getz blocked a punt and Drouilhet picked up the loose ball and ran into the end zone to make the score 6-0. And that's how it stood at the end. Afterward, Tillie Voss, Harvey Long, and Ben Franklin of the Nitehawks were added to the Tigers, and though Bettencourt had broken two fingers, he insisted he would play against the Cardinals and Ernie Nevers.

In this era of triple-threat backs, those who could run, pass, and kick and were required to do so, men who played sixty minutes without substitutions, some without helmets, in the days before the T-Formation made offenses and defenses more complex and specialized, Ernie Nevers was the greatest player in football. He was big (6' 2", 210 pounds), strong, and very fast. Pop Warner, his coach at Stanford University where Nevers had been a great all-American, called him "The greatest all-round back of all-time!" He was also a fine baseball player, having spent three years in the major leagues before joining the Cardinals in 1929. In his rookie season when they played crosstown rival Chicago Bears he scored forty points, a single-game NFL record that has since been approached only once or twice.

The game in Chicago was billed as a matchup between Nevers and Tony Holm, both of whom were recent Rose Bowl heroes, and by Thursday Maxwell, Coyle Shea, and Godman were there to help with the promotion and make last minute arrangements. Along with a few dozen fans, (earlier in the week it was

Cardinals in Comiskey Park

announced in *The Commercial Appeal* that anyone interested in traveling with the team contact Early Maxwell) the Tigers boarded a train on Friday night and arrived in Chicago the next morning. On Sunday in the cavernous stands of Comiskey Park attendance was sparse, and when the Tigers took the field they were outweighed almost fifteen pounds a player.

The game began on a high note for Memphis. The Cardinals' opening drive was stopped, the Tigers took over, and Banker sailed a high punt seventy yards downfield that Bettencourt trapped at the 3-yard line. A few plays later a bad snap from center made Nevers shank his punt, and the ball went out of bounds just yards up the field. So, only minutes into the game, the Tigers had stopped a ferocious offensive drive and were themselves in scoring position. Then they lost control of the game; Banker fumbled, and the Cardinals recovered and drove downfield for a touchdown.

In the second half Nevers showed his great prowess, killing the Tigers' opening drive with an interception deep in his own team's territory, and by the end of the third quarter the Cardinals were ahead 20-0. Their line opened holes through which slipped red-jerseyed runners, and Nevers sprayed the field with bullet passes that found their targets. Bucky Moore at last entered the game in the fourth quarter and ripped off long runs to put the Tigers in scoring position, but Nevers made another interception. The Tigers got the ball back once more and finally scored; Moore caught a pass and was tackled near the goal line, then Simas crashed over on a quarterback sneak. They lost to the Cardinals 6-20. (On this same day in Cincinnati an earlier vanquished foe, the Ironton Tanks, beat the Chicago Bears 32-13.)

The loss was criticized by Stone in the *Memphis Press-Scimitar.*

> BLAME IT ON the folks who ran the Memphis eleven. Why was Bucky Moore kept on the bench until the final quarter? Why didn't Tillie Voss start the game? It was just as well for Ernie Nevers' Chicago Cardinals that Bucky Moore, unhelmeted stick of dynamite, was in the game for only one period. Bucky conducted himself in shattering effect . . . after shining his breeches sliding from one end of the bench to the other.

Tiger officials will not be smart until they line up a certain backfield combination. Any college in the universe would like to have Tony Holm at fullback and Billy Banker and Bucky Moore at halves. There would be no stopping of Moore with interference furnished by Banker and Holm. The three, so far as records show, were not in the lineup at the same time Sunday.

The Tigers' record dropped to 5-2. The week before reports from New York indicated that Doug Wycoff and Ken Strong wanted to return to Memphis. Management replied they had enough good backs already. But when Joe Savoldi, the dark, handsome, all-American fullback at Notre Dame, made himself available, corporate president Coyle Shea, unable to resist the lure of signing a celebrity athlete, sent a telegram north. However, this proved difficult. Shea did not want to strain relations with the NFL, whose rules even then prohibited signing a collegian until his class had graduated. Savoldi's class, though he no longer played for the Irish, had not yet graduated, so the Tigers rescinded their offer. The Bears signed Savoldi instead, creating an uproar that made headlines and causing Joe Carr, the NFL commissioner, to fine Halas $1,000. It turned out not to make much difference for the Bears, though Savoldi made

Good as any anywhere

history in an offhanded manner; not so much for the uproar over his signing, but because it was his misfortune to break in at the same time at the same position on the same team as a rookie from the University of Minnesota named Bronko Nagurski. Subsequently, Savoldi lasted only four games and went to Hollywood to try out for the movies.

The Tigers improved their record to 7-2 by winning two games on the following week. On Thanksgiving Day they routed the Wichita Panthers 45-0 at Southwestern's Fargason Field as Red Strater directed the offense from a Notre Dame shift and, together, Bucky Moore and Shelton rushed for five touchdowns. The Panthers threatened to score only once: they had the ball deep in Tigers' territory when Getz lost his temper and threw a punch, the ball was moved half the distance to the goal line, but the defense held against line plunges and end runs, and the Tigers regained possession. In the final moments, with the stands almost empty, Cavette made a spectacular catch of a long pass from Banker and dashed into the end zone.

Then on Sunday December 1 at Hodges Field they played Mills Stadium from Chicago. It was cold and damp, much rain

Make Local Debut With Tigers vs. Panthers

Ben Franklin (fb)   Harvey Long (lt)   Tillie Voss (re)

New players on the roster

had fallen, and attendance was down. Neither team could do much in the mud. In the second quarter Mills Stadium shanked a punt that sailed over the grandstands onto Jefferson Avenue. Then early in the second half they fumbled at their own 4-yard line, and Cavette pounced on the ball. Two plays later Moore sloughed through a tackle to score. Simas kicked the extra point, and the final score was 7-0.

Prominent In Tiger Victory

Bucky Moore

The players received free tickets to the Warner Theatre on Monday night to see *Maybe Its Love*, a movie starring Joe E. Brown that featured their own Billy Banker as a member of the all-American team. And Maxwell left for Atlanta to complete arrangement for a series against the Brooklyn Dodgers. Meanwhile, Ernie Nevers and the Chicago Cardinals came to Memphis to play on the following Sunday.

The papers boasted that eight former all-Americans, four on the Cardinals and four on the Tigers (Bettencourt, Banker, Moore, and Holm), would be on the field, and advance ticket sales were the highest all season. Nevers arrived at Grand Central Station on Friday morning, December 6. He was met by a crowd of reporters and spent the afternoon speaking before various high school assemblies. His teammates arrived on Saturday, two of whom, tackles Jess Tinsley and Jake Williams, had played for the Tigers in '29, and went directly from the

Maybe Its Love

station to Hodges Field where Nevers lead them through practice. At the same time across the street, the Tigers practiced at Beauregard Field.

The largest crowd all season, 7,000 people, watched under fair skies and mild temperatures. The Cardinals had an explosive offense. Savage line plunged by Nevers and off-tackle dashes by Belden and Maple kept the Tigers on the defensive. But this game was a lot closer than the first one. The Cardinals scored in the second quarter on a reverse from Nevers to Belden and constantly drove down the field. But time after time their drives were checked when Holm or Ben Franklin smeared plays at the line of scrimmage.

Tiger Linesmen Who Open Against Chicago 11 Here Today

Cavette (re),   Ackerman (rt),   Herrin (rg),   Bettencourt (c),   Norvall (lg),   Drouilhet (lt),   Getz (le)

The Line up

Several Tigers were knocked out. An ambulance was called for Woodruff, but he regained consciousness and took a seat on the bench. Bucky Moore twisted an ankle near the end of the first quarter, and thereafter the Tigers could muster no offense. With the game ending just as the Cardinals were stopped inside the 10-yard line, the final score was 0-6.

Nevers left town that night with the promise to return if another game was scheduled. He had declined to play against the Brooklyn Dodgers on the following week, because the Cardinals were already scheduled to play the Bears. But if the Tigers had a post-season game after that, then he would return and join their roster. The Statin Island Stapletons were scheduled for December 21, but they canceled instead to play the New York Giants. It was thought the Bears might replace them, but this did not happen either. Nevers did not return this season. However, he left Memphis on a personal high note as, just before boarding the train, word came to him that Knute Rockne had placed him on the All-Time All-American team.

With two games left in the season, both against the Brooklyn Dodgers on consecutive days, the first one being in Atlanta, team spirit was down. The Tigers had suffered three losses, and lately, in crucial games, the offense had not been productive. One reason was the weather and the wet, slow fields they had played on. Another, and more profound reason, was that the players were divided among themselves. Leadership was split between Bettencourt and Reese. But morale seemed to improve as the week progressed. At Wednesday's practice Strater barked out crisp signals, and the plays were well executed.

They left for Atlanta on Friday morning; that night attending a banquet honoring Brooklyn's Stumpy Thomason, a former all-American at Georgia Tech and the hero of her 1929 Rose Bowl victory over California. Stumpy's teammates arrived the next morning, shedding the fatigue of a long train ride with a brisk workout at Grant Field.

Star of Chicago Cardinals

Ernie Nevers

The Brooklyn Dodgers had finished the NFL season in fourth place with a record of 7-4-1. The game, broadcast back to Memphis, was poorly attended and did not go well for the Tigers. Lacking teamwork and cohesion, their offense was smothered, and on defense the Dodgers blasted through the line for long gains by Thomason and Jake McBride. The Dodgers scored in the first quarter on a pass from Kelly to Algie Clark, and then again in the fourth quarter when Thomason crashed into the end zone. As the final minutes ticked off the clock, behind 0-13, the Tigers threw long, desperate passes that fell incomplete.

The teams met again in Memphis the next day before 1,554 fans. The Tigers, not realizing it was the last game of the season, were a disheartened team. Bettencourt, Ackerman, and Drouil-het sat on the bench nursing minor injuries as the Dodgers dominated the line of scrimmage and took a 13-0 lead. Still, the home team played better than they had in Atlanta. The field was dry, and Moore ran well, nearly breaking loose on a punt return; but he reinjured his ankle and was replaced by Shelton. They lost Banker in the second quarter when his nose was smashed. Gil Reese, making his first appearance as a Tiger since 1927, entered the game in the fourth quarter and dashed off a few long runs and kept down the score with flying tackles. The Ti-gers made thirteen first downs during the game but failed to penetrate Brooklyn's 30-yard line, and toward the end fights broke out. Getz and Tomaini of Brooklyn were ejected. When the final gun went off, the Tigers' record had dropped to 7-5.

Two Brooklyn Ends Tigers Face Here Sunday

Bob Mahan
(Washington University of St. Louis)

Earl Plank
(Ohio State)

Brooklyn Ends

Stone wrote in *The Commercial Appeal*, "It was hard on fans who sat back and watched the Dodgers twist Tiger Tails. It was sad, too." And he asked, "Smatter with the Tigers this year? They looked as good on paper as they did in 1929 when they beat the Green Bay Packers for the National Championship." And answered, "The 1930 Tigers have no Ken Strong nor Doug Wycoff . . . I believe Tiger officials blundered in not bringing them on." But he finished on a positive, generous note, "Regardless of recent defeats the Tigers provided fine entertainment for local grid enthusiasts. We hope they'll be back next year."

But the problem of recent defeats was perplexing, and on Tuesday Stone printed a caustic letter from a fan: "Your column telling why the Tigers finished second best in their last game is all wet. How do you expect a team to sign high-salaried men like Ken Strong and Doug Wycoff when a city doesn't support it? Real trouble is the club has too many bosses! What do you think?"

"Too many bosses," replied Stone. "I'll grant you that . . . There were more huddles on the Tiger Bench than there were on the field. Gil Reese knows football. He was educated by Uncle Daniel McGugin at Vanderbilt where he played remarkable football. I believe you would have seen a smarter Tiger team had Gil been put in complete charge of the team on the playing field." But he still disagreed about Strong and Wycoff. "I confess Tiger officials would not have been smart had they increased their already top-heavy payroll. But there was a way around. The roster was too big . . . Why couldn't enough of the 'Dead Timber' been axed off to pay salaries demanded by Strong and Wycoff?"

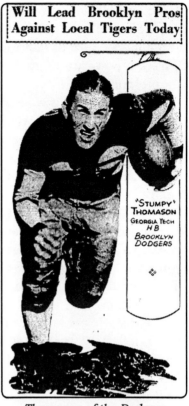

Will Lead Brooklyn Pros Against Local Tigers Today

"Stumpy" Thomason
Georgia Tech
HB
Brooklyn
Dodgers

Thomason of the Dodgers

However, some of the problems went deeper than the public realized. Early in the season the St. Mary's players had formed a clique among themselves, and then they and some of the others grumbled over Billy Banker not practicing during the week. Bettencourt had let these things fester. The real problem with the Tigers, as was suggested in the fans' letter, had been in the leadership. A big winner, and they had the kind of players to produce one, would have made the public a lot more receptive.

It snowed on Tuesday December 16, and the temperature dropped below freezing. Officers of the corporation met in Godman's office in the Sterick Building at noon and declared that the season was over. "Weather is too threatening to even consider carrying on another week or two," Maxwell told reporters.

But there was more business to be considered. Minneapolis was quitting the NFL after suffering through a dismal season, and their franchise was offered to Memphis for $3,000. With elated expectation, Maxwell told the press, "We'll retain options on all players now on our roster . . . We're already negotiating with college stars of last fall and present NFL stars. We expect to have a powerful team next fall and win that National League Championship!"

Another meeting was scheduled at Godman's office to discuss the proposal, but when the time came Coyle Shea was ill, and the meeting was postponed until Christmas Eve. In the meantime, the accounting firm of James Mathews & Co. delivered the financial statements to the board of directors. The Memphis Professional Football Association had lost $13,500 and was $5,000 in debt. In fact, after the last game they had to borrow money to pay player salaries, nor was there even enough money to pay their expenses home, a stipulation written into contracts. Among the debts incurred was a $17.50 advertising bill owed to young Kemmons Wilson, who years later founded Holiday Inns.

The meeting that was to have taken place on Christmas Eve was indefinitely postponed and never occurred. The men were indifferent due to financial difficulty; and a great opportunity, one presently much desired by the city, was lost. On the following July at an annual meeting of the NFL held in the Edgewater Beach Hotel in Chicago, Joe Carr was elected to another term as commissioner and cities petitioning for membership were Cincinnati, Cleveland, and Milwaukee. There was no one there representing Memphis.

Maxwell's Pride

NUTE ROCKNE took a train from Chicago to Kansas City where on March 31, 1931, he boarded a Ford Trimotor flying to Los Angeles. The weather was bad, as storms brewed across the Great Plains. The plane landed in Wichita, then continued on its fateful journey, flying through heavy rain and winds, and crashed into a field outside of a place named Bazaar, Kansas. Rockne, five other passengers, and the crew perished. The shock of his death lingered and was keenly felt in the fall. There were commitments and rededications and reviews of the past. The death of a hero is a sobering and introspective ordeal.

Nineteen thirty-one was a vintage year for professional football in Memphis. The Tigers learned from the mistakes of the previous year and made their finest effort. Early Maxwell, in relentless pursuit of a dream, was the heart and drive. The coaching problem was solved by hiring one of the best athletes the city had yet produced: Goat Hale, who was a graduate of Christian Brothers, where his younger brother Marion had just been named the new coach, and had gone on to play football at Mississippi College in Starkville. He first coached at the high school in Poplarville, Mississippi, where under his tutelage Bucky Moore had developed into a running back hailed as "The greatest ever produced in the South," and then at Millsaps College in Jackson, Mississippi, where his teams were noted for their passing and, he, for being an inspired leader. Though nearing thirty, Hale was still fast and in playing shape. Perhaps

Leader of Local Pros

BUSY MOORE

"DIXIE FLYER"
CAPTAIN-TIGERS

Bucky returns

Veteran in Tiger Line

Austin Applewhite (RE)

Austin Applewhite, right end of the Memphis Tigers professional eleven making ready for an engagement with Louisville at Hodges Field next Sunday, is one of the veterans of the local pros. Applewhite, former captain of the University of Mississippi gridiron forces, joined the Saunders Tigers in 1929 and was one of the big stars in the victory over Green Bay Packers, National League champions. He got off to a fine start this season when the Tigers licked Dayton, Ohio, Guards here two weeks ago.

Austin Applewhite

Two Hopes of the Tigers

Jess Eberdt (Center)   Joe Moore (Tackle)
(Alabama)   (Arkansas)

New Tiger linemen

it was for this reason that Bucky Moore spurned offers from the Green Bay Packers and Chicago Cardinals to once again return to Memphis. After several years apart, coach and player would be reunited in the same backfield.

Maxwell quickly organized the squad. He announced he wanted a team comprised exclusively of players from the South, and this was almost totally achieved. He tried and failed to sign Memphis Chicks' slugger Joe Hutcheson, who wanted to play but was refused permission by club president Tom Watkins Sr. Bettencourt would not be back. It was reported that he was about to sign with an NFL team (he would, in fact, eventually spend two seasons with the Green Bay Packers), then it was reported he had organized his own team in St. Louis, where he had just finished his first season of major league baseball as an outfielder for the St. Louis Browns and was looking for a game against the Tigers. Jess Eberdt (6' 1", 215 pounds), bigger than Bettencourt and a starter for three years at Alabama under coach Wallace Wade, was signed to take his place at center. The only man from St. Mary's to return was Hoot Herrin.

Cavette, Norvell, Shelton, and Applewhite were back, along with Duke Kimbrough. And there were two new men from the University of Arkansas, 180-pound fullback Garland Beavers and 230-pound tackle Joe Moore, who would figure prominently during the season. However, the business community was not responding to pleas for support, and Maxwell told the press that without adequate financial backing, the Tigers would be forced to play all their games on the road. It was a threat he would make often throughout the season.

Their first practice was held under the arc lights at Hodges Field on Monday evening, September 28, with less than a week before the first game of the season. The players went through calisthenics and then lined up in punt formation. "City" Thomason, a former Southwestern star, snapped the ball from center as several men took turns kicking. Naylor Stone, watching from the sidelines, wrote the next day, "No college team ever worked harder its first time out. Hale is working with some fine looking material."

On Sunday they played the Dayton Guards, considered one of the best teams outside the NFL. The Guards had won seven

Big Bill Thompson of Chicago

games the previous year, but were not very big, averaging about 190-pounds a player. The game was promoted as "Jess Eberdt Day," and people from his nearby hometown of Blytheville, Arkansas, made the trip to see him play. Sitting close to the field on the 50-yard line were two prominent mayors: Chicago's legendary "Big Bill" Thompson and Arthur O'Keefe of New Orleans, who were in town conferring about the future of river transportation between their two cities. Behind them sat Clarence Saunders with his young, pretty bride.

The skies were threatening, a brief shower fell before kickoff, and the Tigers blocked with clockwork precision, in the second quarter mounting a long drive with Beavers vaulting into the end zone. But the game was close until the final period when Dayton's efforts collapsed. Applewhite returned an interception fifty-seven yards for a touchdown, and Moore followed up with a sprint around right end from twenty-five yards out. The reserves came off the bench. Schneider carried down to the 7-yard line, and Leftwich scored on the next play. The Tigers won 26-0. Any profit from the game, which had not been well attended, was split among the players and Maxwell.

REAL ACTION IN PRO-GRID INAUGURAL YESTERDAY AT HODGES FIELD

Action on the field

There was no game on the following Sunday. Maxwell told the press, "The schedule will not have more than three games arranged ahead of time at any stage in order to assure the best opposition possible." But, in fact, for the weeks ahead no games had been scheduled at all. It seemed like professional football in Memphis had already come to an end.

The times were hard. The Great Depression, about to enter its third year, cast a lengthening shadow. Businesses failed and unemployment rose drastically. There was not much money in professional football, yet the Tigers continued practicing, and Maxwell talked to other teams. The roster had twenty players, most of them living in boarding houses along Jefferson Avenue and without jobs to work during the day. Cavette and Norvell, working for the railroad, were among the few regularly employed. Then, at last, the barren landscape yielded more water. A game was scheduled against the Crescent Hill club of Louisville for Sunday October 18.

At the Orpheum on Tuesday night the players watched The Spirit of Notre Dame, featuring The Four Horsemen as themselves. Crescent Hill arrived on Saturday morning with twenty-eight players and quartered at the Chisca Hotel. At noon Shelton and Moore, along with two Crescent Hill backs, spoke over the radio. The Tigers made changes to their lineup: Kimbrough had injured his ankle so sturdy, little Hoot Herrin was moved to right tackle and Loady Blankenbacker took over at right guard. On Sunday the game quickly turned into a rout.

In the first quarter Bucky Moore broke loose and scored twice on long runs; the second time on a punt return, squirming and stiff-arming his way fifty-three yards into the end zone. At the end of the period the score was 20-0 and the reserves came off the bench. The Tigers moved the ball almost at will and won easily, 39–0.

They needed better competition almost as badly as they needed money. When the players showed up to get paid on Monday there was not much to go around. Maxwell again threatened to take them on the road. The payroll and expenses could be met by guarantees, he said, and though such an arrangement might cost a few good players, he thought the Tigers could still be able to battle any team in the country. The next game was against the Milwaukee Nitehawks. To meet their guarantee and rent the stadium, $2,000 was needed. The Shelby County

Bucky Moore (qb)
(Tigers)

Mendelsohn (qb)
(Nitehawks)

Game Captains

With Tigers
In "Comeback"

May Rejoin
Tiger Pros

Red Schneider   Fred Getz

Athletic Commission issued a proclamation urging support of
the Tigers. "If Milwaukee cannot draw here then we might as
well check out!" said Maxwell. But advance ticket sales were
good, and over 2,000 people showed up at Hodges Field on a
warm Sunday afternoon.

The Tigers played outstanding defense. Cavette blocked a
field goal attempt when the Nitehawks made their only scoring threat. But Memphis could not get their aerial attack working, and the Nitehawks, playing good defense, too, checked
their drives. Eberdt ripped holes in the line for Beavers to plow
through, and five times they threatened to score, but each time
were turned back. Then Red Schneider, who had been cut from
the squad in 1930, made his comeback as a player complete. In

the fourth quarter Beavers was knocked out and carried off the field. Schneider replaced him and with less than three minutes remaining he plunged into the end zone for 6–0 victory. Just as important, over $3,100 had been collected at the gates. The Nitehawks complained that the heat had made them sluggish and left town wanting a rematch.

Things looked better. Stone wrote on Monday, "While there aren't as many standout stars on the Tigers this year as there were last, they are better balanced, better conditioned, and a stronger club. I've never seen a smoother running pro outfit."

The next game was against the Hominey Indians, a traditionally good draw. But the roster needed patching. Shelton and

In Lineups Of Tigers and Indians Today

(Left)—Captain Harding (guard) Indians. (Center)—Jess Eberdt (center) Tigers. (Right)—Davis (end) Indians.

Indians Play Today

Cavette were limping, and Norvell's eye was scratched. Also, the Tigers needed more weight to match up against the Indians, whose line averaged 226 pounds. Maxwell signed a professional wrestler named Blue Sun Jenning, who had played with the Chicago Cardinals in 1930, and when Bucky Moore, Kimbrough, and Eberdt were offered contracts in the NFL, he persuaded them to stay.

Tickets went on sale at Fortune-Ward Drugs. The Indians arrived Saturday morning, and in the afternoon practiced at Hodges Field during the halftime of a prep game. (Maxwell rarely missed an opportunity for free promotion.) One of the Indians, Chief Fixico, played without a helmet and shoulder pads, a sight becoming less and less common.

On Sunday attendance was up, though the stands were not crowded. The Tigers received the opening kickoff, drove down the field, and Beavers crashed into the end zone. It was the only score of the game. The Indians were ponderous, but their linemen stayed fresh with frequent substituting, and they bottled up Bucky Moore. In the second half a fleet Indian halfback took a lateral and bolted fifty-six yards until Applewhite caught him from behind to make a game-saving tackle. The game ended in darkness with the final score 6-0.

Maxwell scheduled the Indians again for the following Sunday, but canceled later in the week because too many players were injured, and left for Chicago on Friday November 6. The undefeated and unscored-upon Tigers, resting on their hard-earned laurels and recuperating, were praised in *The Commercial Appeal*:

WITH SMOOTHER teamwork and a stronger defense, the Tigers have improved over the 1930 outfit. Though some All-American stars are lacking they are not missed. With the exception of Clarence Saunders' Tigers that beat the Green Bay Packers and Chicago Bears in 1929, the present Tigers compose the strongest eleven in the five year history of pro football here.

They had captured the imagination of the press; albeit, Maxwell had much influence on the city's sports reporters, and

As 'Chain' Attack Scores For Tigers

Action against the Indians

there was auspicious speculation about possible opponents in the near future. Stone wrote,

EARLY MAXWELL SHOULD bring the New York Giants here. The Giants probably have the greatest set of backs in football today. Benny Friedman, the old Michigan All-American star, is at quarterback. Red Cagle of Army fame and Jack Burnett, who starred at Southern Methodist University, are halfbacks and Doug Wycoff, former Tigers and All-American at Georgia Tech, is at fullback.

The *Memphis Press-Scimitar* reported that a charity game in Knoxville was being negotiated and, if scheduled, the opponent would be either the Chicago Cardinals or a team from New Orleans led by Billy Banker. If so, then Maxwell wanted Gene McEver and Buddy Hackman, the touchdown twins of Tennessee, to play in the Tigers' backfield. Then on Sunday *The Commercial Appeal* wrote, "The Bears will most likely be brought here."

Maxwell did negotiate with Giants' owner Tim Mara, and in Chicago, after watching the Bears beat the Portsmouth Spartans, he talked to Halas. But the guarantees they wanted were too high. However, he was able to set up late-season games

Former All-American Will Coach Against Tigers Here

Chick Harley, former All-American, with Ohio State signing contract to coach Mills Stadium team of Chicago managed by his brother (standing) Bill Harley.

The Harley Brothers

against two NFL teams, the Cardinals and the Providence Steamrollers, opened the door for other possibilities, and scheduled Mills Stadium for the following week.

Mills Stadium's new coach had a storied past that was badly marred by an entanglement with Halas. In 1920 Chick Harley was the most renown name in college football, having been a Walter Camp all-American at Ohio State in 1917 and again in 1919, and Halas and Sternaman were able to sign him only after giving him and his brother part ownership of the Bears. But the Harleys, not satisfied with the final contract, tore it up, incensing the already tenacious Halas and Sternaman.

Chick played for the Bears, but within a year was cut from the roster and removed from the payroll. Claiming mental harassment, the Harleys took legal action. When the case came to court, the judge asked Sternaman to state the net value of the Bears. Sternaman shrugged and replied, "Eleven jocks in the locker room." The case drifted into oblivion, so did the Harleys' claim to part ownership of the Bears, and Chick had a nervous breakdown and spent several months in a sanitarium.

In Memphis, Whitey Shelton was kicked off the Tigers' roster because of an indifference to practice and other unspecified rule infractions. Hale replaced him with a halfback from Millsaps named Jackie Miller. Miller was already well-known in the area, because in the clash of rivalries in the fall of 1929 at Fargason Field on the Southwestern campus, it was he who had scored the winning touchdown for Millsaps against Southwestern.

Mills Stadium Stars

Rain fell across the country, and in Chicago, Mills Stadium practiced in the mud. They could extend their season with a victory over the Tigers and arrived in Memphis on Saturday afternoon with nineteen highly motivated players. The rain stopped by Sunday, and 2,000 people were in the stands. On the Tigers' bench sat a penitent Whitey Shelton in civilian clothes.

The game was scoreless and close throughout. Mills Stadium played well on defense, displaying swiftness and coordination, the best attributes of a small team, but was smothered on offense. The Tigers were not without punch, Schneider broke loose on a forty-five-yard run; and in the second half they settled into the running pattern of Beavers behind Eberdt's blocks, and mounted a drive that took them within one foot of the goal line. But Mills Stadium rallied, and the Tigers lost the ball on downs. The visitors escaped with a tie; contracts were offered to two of their players, but each was turned down. A rematch was scheduled in two weeks.

Changes were made to the lineup during the week; too many of the players were walking around wounded. Norvell had a dislocated shoulder, Herrin a sprained ankle, and Joe Moore's leg was hurt. So Applewhite was moved to left tackle, and Jimmy Tarr from Indiana took over right end. Bucky Moore, quarterbacking the last few games, returned to his natural position at halfback, and Hale moved Leftwich to quarterback and on Thursday reinstated Shelton. Rain forced the team to practice indoors.

"Bucky" Moore Making One Of His Gains For Tigers

Bucky Moore carries the mail

Detroit's giant Stingari

The next opponent, the Detroit Collegians, had a long string of victories and was the self-proclaimed professional champions of Michigan. They sneaked into town on Friday morning thirty-six hours ahead of schedule and practiced in the mud at Hodges Field. This galvanized the Tigers, who wanted to keep their unbeaten record intact for late-season games against NFL teams, and they also held an unscheduled practice outdoors that night. Norvell, who weighed only 190 pounds, disregarded his injuries so that he could play against Charles Stingari, Detroit's 253-pound tackle.

They played on a day, Sunday November 22, that was unseasonably warm with temperatures rising to 78 degrees. Kickoff was moved forward fifteen minutes to prevent the game from finishing in darkness. The Tigers proved to be quicker on the field, stopping the slow Detroit backs at the line of scrimmage and easily solving their aerial attack with three interceptions. But Detroit played good defense, rallying whenever the Tigers crossed midfield, and the advantage went to the team with the best field position.

In the second half the Tigers' Larry Marks returned the kickoff sixty yards, then a pass from Moore to Cavette and two running plays took the Tigers to the 2-yard line, where they lost the ball on downs. But Detroit shanked the ensuing punt, and the Tigers took over at the 17-yard line. Moore ripped off five yards, and on the next play handed the ball to Billy Murray on a reverse, and Murray scampered around left end for a

Two Of Backfield Hopes Of Tigers Against Detroit

Larry Marks (hb).   Garland Beavers (fb).

Tiger backfield against Detroit

touchdown. That was all that was needed. The Collegians were vanquished 6-0.

Amidst the city's bustle and preparation for the coming Yuletide season, with 125,000 people jamming the sidewalks along Main Street for the annual Christmas Parade on the last Saturday of November, the Mills Stadium professional football team was hardly noticed when they returned on the following Saturday. Tony Udovich (6' 1", 210 pounds) from the Nitehawks had been added to the Tigers' roster and reported to the team on Friday. He was quickly tried at several positions in practice before it was decided to start him at guard. During the Christmas Parade the sky was dark and threatening, then rain began to fall. It rained hard throughout Sunday, cutting attendance to less than 1,000.

The field was a sea of mud. The players quickly became dark figures indistinguishable from one another, and the few fans there found it comic and inversely delightful. The ball was like a greased pig and fumbled nineteen times. But Garland Beavers, whose picture had appeared in Friday's *Commercial Appeal*, proved a master at kicking a slick ball and pinned down Mills Stadium on their 2-yard line with a long punt in the second

Udovich added to the roster

quarter. Larry Foley of Mills Stadium then lost his grip on the ball, and the Tigers crashed through and smothered him for a safety. It grew dark early, the lights were turned on in the third quarter, and the Tigers took control of the game. Settling into quarterback, Beavers completed two passes, then they ran for a touchdown, and the final score was 8-0.

But there was only enough money to meet the visiting team's guarantee, and the Tigers went unpaid. Stone wrote in

Garland Beavers

the *Memphis Press-Scimitar*, "Early Maxwell deserves a lot of credit for keeping professional football staggering along tho' he had no backers and poor crowds compared with those of other years". The city's interest in pro football was at a lull, however, team spirits were still up. On Tuesday several players were on the streets downtown soliciting for the Community Fund. And Stone wrote, "Tho the Tigers are behind in expenses and cannot engage in a benefit game, the local professionals are doing their part for charity."

Practice was canceled on Wednesday. The players had the choice between attending a funeral (Billy Murray's father, a local doctor, had died) or traveling to Blytheville, Arkansas, for Jess

Ebert gets married

Eberdt's marriage to his high-school sweetheart. (Bucky Moore served as groomsman.) This year they were a team both on and off the field and, at last, having found a good quarterback in Garland Beavers, were about to play their best football of the year. Duke Kimbrough, who had been confined with the flu to his bed in Mississippi, and Cliff Norvell returned to the lineup. The men practiced outdoors despite the rain on Thursday and

With Kansas City Cowboys Against Tigers Here Today

Sivers (Qu.)
(New Mexico Univ.)

Moran (G.)
(North Carolina State)

Cheatam (Hb.)
(Baker Univ.)

The Cowboys

again held a spirited workout Saturday morning. The *Memphis Press-Scimitar* reported that "They appeared in the veritable pink [of physical condition]."

The Kansas City Cowboys came to town with a string of victories against lackluster competition, and after weeks of lethargy the Tigers' offense exploded. They amassed twenty-six first downs, Beavers threw five touchdown passes, and in the final period scored twenty-six points using mostly reserves. (Eberdt had left the field at the end of the first quarter.) The Cowboys were stunned, few people remained in the stands, only about 1,500 were there at the start, as the final score was 64-0.

Thus far in the season only two teams, Milwaukee and Mills Stadium, had even penetrated the Tigers' 15-yard line. Coming up were games against NFL teams (Maxwell rejected an offer from the Portsmouth Spartans, one of the NFL's best teams, because on the date they wanted he had already scheduled the Chicago Cardinals), but first, in a move that Maxwell came to regret, they scheduled a game on Saturday December 12, the day before they were to play the Providence Steamrollers, against Bonneycastle in Louisville.

The National Football League, not yet divided into conferences, had ten teams in 1931. The Providence Steamrollers of

Tigers Claim National Independent Pro Football Crown

Tiger claim title

Rhode Island, finishing the season in sixth place with a 4-4-1 record, had one of the best passing combinations in pro football, Dexter Shelley to Glenn Rose, and their line, with two all-pros from the year before, was big and experienced. Tickets went on sale Wednesday morning at Ambrose Sporting Goods and Fortune-Ward Drugstore. And though the Steamrollers were given the largest guarantee of the season and would travel the furthest distance to play the Tigers, Maxwell made it clear in a letter printed in the *Memphis Press-Scimitar* that the cost of admission would be the same as for all other games: general admission, $1.50; reserved seats, $2.50; and box seats, $3.00.

On Thursday the Tiger ends, Applewhite and Cavette, were pictured in *The Commercial Appeal* wearing jerseys and knee breeches: Applewhite stood erect with his hands hanging not so loosely down his sides, and Cavette was crouched and leaned forward with his right hand on the ground for balance. The Tigers finished their last practice of the week "in the veritable pink" and boarded a train to Louisville on Friday night. At about the same time as they were leaving, an early contingent of Steamrollers lead by Cowboy Woodruff, who had helped arrange the game, arrived by car and scheduled a practice at Hodges Field for the following afternoon.

Bonneycastle was viewed as a warm-up game and played mostly by reserves. Garland Beavers, in Arkansas coaching a high school team, did not even make the trip. The game started in a drizzle that turned into a downpour, and the attendance was sparse. The Tigers took a 6-0 lead on a run by Moore. And then, on a controversial play in the second quarter, had the first points scored against them all season: Bonneycastle punted, and when the ball rolled into the Tigers' end zone, Moore apparently touched it, Billy Murray picked it up, and was tackled for a safety. But Moore disputed the call, yelling at the officials for five minutes, until the referee ruled that the ball had been touched and awarded the points to Bonneycastle. The Tigers

All-National Pro League Center Plays Here Sunday

Ray Smith.

Smith of Providence Will Oppose Eberdt Here Sunday

Former University of Missouri Star With Steamrollers in Lineup Against Unbeaten Memphis Tigers at Hodges Field.

Opposing center

scored again after a long, galloping run by Moore set up a short run by Marks into the end zone. And Bonneycastle scored another safety, this time without argument. The team left Louisville late in the evening and returned to Memphis with a 12-4 victory, the dismal weather following them.

On Sunday the rain alternated between a drizzle and a downpour. Less than 1,000 fans attended the game, blustery winds making them shiver. The Steamrollers pushed the Tigers all over the hard and slippery field as Shelley passed to Meeker for one touchdown and to Rose for another and took a 12-0 halftime lead. But the Tigers pulled themselves together in the second half as Beaver's long punts gave them good field position, and in the fourth quarter Bucky Moore hit his stride, returning a punt to the Providence 20, where three plays later he cut through right tackle to score.

The lights were turned on, the field took on a sheen, and the Tigers were ready to take the lead when Cavette recovered a blocked punt at the Providence 3-yard line. But on an end sweep Jackie Miller was hit so hard that he fumbled, and Providence recovered. The Tigers got the ball back and were again in Providence territory, but Beavers became too cautious and time ran out. They lost to the Steamrollers 6-12. Maxwell claimed remorsefully that the game in Louisville and the long train ride through the night had taken the edge off his team.

"Until Saturday the local pro team had not been scored upon all year," wrote Stone on Tuesday afternoon. "If they had gotten by Sunday, it would have been a pretty safe bet they wouldn't have been scored upon the rest of the season. Acquisition of Ken Strong, one of the greatest back in the country, and Cowboy Woodruff, a brilliant line plunger, has turned the Tigers from a good into a great machine."

Ken Strong had just been married on Saturday night, and the drive down from New York was his honeymoon. He and his bride reached Memphis on Tuesday, the same day as Ernie Nevers, who arrived that evening at Grand Central Station after his teammates. Nevers had been in St. Louis, where on Sunday the Cardinals had played an exhibition game before 12,000 people. He had stayed behind to complete arrangements for a West Coast tour in January. Immediately, a series of radio interviews

Ken Strong

were set up with him and Strong. Nevers and Strong had never played against each other, nor had they even met. Strong told reporters that the Tigers had a better chance of beating the Cardinals than did his Stapleton Club.

Although they had not won the NFL title, the Chicago Cardinals were considered to be the best team in professional football. After a poor start, playing under a coach whom none of the players liked, Nevers took over at midseason, and they began to win impressively, beating the eventual champion Green Bay Packers late in the season and finishing with a 5-4 record.

Along with Nevers, center Art McNally was named to the all-pro team. They also had two small, speedy halfbacks named Bunny Beldon and Gene Rose, known as "The Pony Backfield," who made their offense dangerous and versatile.

The Tigers, buoyed by last Sunday's showing against Providence, were confident and concentrated well in practice. But Maxwell was gloomy and worried about the weather. With the trip to Louisville fresh in his mind, he turned down an offer to play in New Orleans on Saturday. Rain on the last two Sundays had kept crowds away from the games, and the rain continued to fall. Sand and straw were placed over the field at Hodges, and Maxwell moved practices across the street to Beauregard Field. Crowds gathered there to watch in the afternoons.

On Wednesday the Cardinals scrimmaged against a squad of policemen. Then on Thursday the cloud cover began to break, brilliant shafts of December sun slanted through, and the air chilled and cooled, becoming cold. With Christmas only a week away and two of the world's greatest football players in town, midtown took on the atmosphere of a carnival. Hundreds of fans swarmed the sidewalks and street corners as, first, the Cardinals took to the practice field, setting a furious pace with red jerseys moving precisely as Nevers barked out orders, then, when it was the Tigers' turn, Strong would punt the ball almost out of sight.

The papers predicted the outcome a tossup and rated Strong and Nevers even on punting and passing. The difference between them was in their running styles. Strong excelled in

Nevers Shows No Respect For 'Law'

—Press-Scimitar Photo

Ernie Nevers and his Chicago Cardinals showed flagrant disrespect for the "law" Friday at Beauregard Field. Above they are shown working their vaunted passing attack in scrimmage with Memphis police eleven. Nevers has faded out of the picture, going back to shoot a pass to Kassell, end, No. 40, at the extreme right. John Getz, who is coaching the policemen, is just behind Kassell, attempting to knock down the heave.

Cardinals practice in silhouette

The Cardinal game

the open field, but Nevers was stronger and worked behind the better line.

Both men were out among the public during the week. Nevers appeared before the student assembly of Tech High School and told them that Red Grange was the greatest player he had ever played against, adding that when he and Jim Thorpe were once on opposing teams, Thorpe had been well past his prime. Finally, the men were formally introduced to each other by Early Maxwell over his radio show on Friday night.

As for the game itself, with high expectations the Tigers were planning a familiar strategy: hold Bucky Moore out of the starting lineup, then rush him into the game when the Cardinals were worn down by the battering runs of Woodruff and Strong. But none of this would matter, it would not go this way, because on Sunday the Cardinals played so well that defeat was an irrefutable conclusion to a harsh, methodical process. The Tigers' plays were smeared, and their ball carriers dropped for losses.

The weather was balmy at the start, and 3,000 people were in the stands. Ken Strong, ineffective as a runner this day, limped onto the field with his left leg heavily taped and booted the opening kickoff into the opposite end zone. The Cardinals promptly marched down the field and scored two touchdowns in the first quarter. The Tigers made one drive down to the Cardinals' goal line, but then bogged down in a shower of rain. In the second half the Cardinals poured it on.

Bunny Belden returned a punt sixty-five yards for a touchdown; the last one to have a shot at him was Ken Strong, himself, and he missed in a headlong sprawl. Then they blocked a punt deep in Tiger territory, and Nevers bucked the line, finally going off tackle to make the score 0-24. With a terrible shutout looming in the waning minutes, Beavers found Miller alone at the 50-yard line and, like a bolt of lightning from a clear, blue sky, threw for a touchdown to make the final score 6-24. Ernie Nevers had played the entire sixty minutes and rushed for over 100 yards.

There were offers to play more games, but on Christmas Eve Maxwell announced, "The game with Nevers took an edge off anything we could bring now . . . Nevers succeeded in climaxing the local season with a great exhibition."

The season had been run on a shoestring budget, but the players stuck with Maxwell and finished with a record of 8-2-1. Any money that was made, and some games made nothing, was evenly divided. The books were balanced, and every visiting team had been paid their full guarantee. On the last Sunday of the year, December 27, *The Commercial Appeal* paid tribute: "One of the best professional football teams in the history of the sport here represented the city."

Hot Rod Backfield

*M*AXWELL disassociated himself from professional football and returned to his old job as sportswriter. There was not enough money to keep him involved. But the Tigers continued on, riding the momentum of a winning tradition, and in 1932 turned in another fine performance on the field.

George Treadwell was named club president, and on September 20 announced that New Brys Department Store would once again sponsor professional football in Memphis. Two days later, on a Thursday evening, Monk Godman and Goat Hale took the train to Chicago, where they obtained a list of players soon available when the NFL trimmed its rosters. "Players from all parts of the country want positions on the team," Treadwell told the press, and ambitiously offered contracts to former Tennessee Vol greats Gene McEver and Herman Hickman, which neither accepted.

However, much talent was assembled, and a lot of it came from the NFL. When Gene Rose left the Cardinals to try out for the Tigers, Frosty Peters came with him; both men, dissatisfied with the new Cardinal coach, were established veterans who had already played three games of the current season. At his first practice Rose told reporters, "I think there is a great future for pro football in the South, especially in Memphis." And Peters was a dropkick artist with a prominent friend in town named Walter Stewart, sports editor of the *Memphis Press-Scimitar*, who had once been his teammate at the University of Illinois.

Stewart wrote,

PETERS IS ONE of the smartest quarters ever turned out by the astute Bob Zuppke. He once beat Ohio State by scooping up the ball on the one foot line and diving over just as the gun was fired to end the game. . . . The writer has seen him stand on the 50-yard line, dropkick a goal, turn around and put another over the goal at the opposite end of the field. Frosty used to send dropkicks spinning down the field for 50 or 60 yards . . . The Chicago Cardinals are getting rid of their [Pop] Warner [system] trained men as the team has taken up the Notre Dame system thus giving the Tigers the chance to sign Peters. The Tigers are growing steadily stronger and if the management continues to sign grade A material, Memphians will be proud of their pro gridders.

The line was beefed up by adding Danny McMullen (6' 2", 225 pounds) from the Chicago Bears and Clyde Van Sickle (6' 1", 220 pounds) from the Green Bay Packers. Over the protest of Godman they signed Larry Bettencourt. At the end of 1930 Bettencourt had left town without returning in a Ford Model A that

The Dayton Guards

was half owned by the team. "We wouldn't pay him a nickel to play here. We do not want him!" exclaimed Godman. But it was thought that he might be a draw at the gate and a contract was offered over a long distance phone call to St. Louis, which he accepted. Another player added was former Ole Miss fullback Solly Cohen, who arrived well overweight at 250 pounds.

During the first week of October they practiced twice a day to prepare for the first game of the season. On Tuesday night under the arc lights at Hodges a sudden drop in temperature added zest to the players' movements. The next morning they showed up looking splendid in orange and black jerseys with leather helmets to match. Hale moved them up and down the field in snappy football formations. The *Memphis Press-Scimitar* wrote, "Power, versatility, and speed are there in profuse quantities." But Bettencourt had not yet arrived. He was reportedly delayed by a car wreck, and when he did finally arrive he failed to show up at practice.

The Tigers opened the season on Sunday October 9 against the Dayton Guards, stronger this year with bigger players. On Saturday morning Hale tried to find Bettencourt. He had checked out of his hotel room and left no forwarding address. So at noon it was announced that he was off the team; his place at center to be taken by "City" Thomason. But this was not yet the end of Larry Bettencourt. In a few weeks he would show up as an opposing player.

On Sunday morning the Tigers were pictured in the sports section of *The Commercial Appeal.* Their jerseys, dark at the shoulders and arms, had "BRYS" written across the front. Van Sickle loomed like a big monster in the middle of the second

Tickets on sale

Bry's Tigers, Local Pro Eleven, Which Makes Debut Today

1932 Tigers

row. Goat Hale stood on the far right. On the front row were eight men, each with one knee on the ground. Cool temperatures were forecasted, and that afternoon they defeated the Dayton Guards 28-0. Frosty Peters was the star.

Walter Stewart had written, "Peters is a great passer and can lug the oval with the best." And in the first quarter he threw a fifty-yard touchdown pass to Cavette and galloped thirty-two yards on a punt return. In the second quarter Rose dashed fifteen yards from scrimmage, then caught a pass to put the ball on Dayton's 12-yard line where Cohen, a very strong man, plunged into the line four successive times, at last waddling into the end zone to make the score 13-0 at half time.

Cohen scored again on a line plunge in the third quarter, and Peters dropkicked a thirty-five-yard field goal. Then in the fourth quarter Punch McDaniels intercepted a Dayton pass and returned it to the 5-yard line, where Rose dashed in on the next play. Dayton showed some offense in the final minutes by driving seventy yards downfield, but was halted at the Tigers' 15-yard line. The Tigers took over, and, with Cohen ramming and Peters passing, only the clock aborted another score. But attendance was disappointing. "It hurt the gate when fans learned that Bettencourt would not play," wrote *Memphis Press-Scimitar* columnist Bob Pigue.

Hodges Field was booked on the following Sunday with a prep game, and efforts to bring in the St. Louis Gunners on Friday night failed. The next game scheduled was against the

Local Pro Backs Against St. Louis Tomorrow

GENE ROSE
(H.B.) Wisc

FROSTY PETERS
(H.B.) Ill

Peters and Rose

Milwaukee Nitehawks for October 23; but then that game was postponed to November 20, the St. Louis Warriors taking their place. Meanwhile, Godman stirred up some controversy in an attempt to sign Papa Felts, the Tulane football captain who had been ruled ineligible for collegiate play after it was discovered he had played professional baseball back in 1927. Felts was not interested in playing for the Tigers, but Jim Pederson, another NFL veteran who had spent the past three years running interference for Red Grange out of the Bears' backfield, was signed. And they also acquired 230-pound guard Al Culver from the Packers, however briefly, for over the weekend when the NFL raised its roster limit from twenty to twenty-two players, Culver returned to the Packers.

Changes to the roster for the upcoming game continued with Art Parisien, a highly touted quarterback from Notre Dame, being cut from the squad. Gerald Seiberling, a halfback from the Bears who had injured his leg, was allowed to stay on because he had a good throwing arm. And at Tuesday's practice Cavette suffered a painful shoulder injury and was replaced in the lineup by a big deaf-mute named Dummy Monahan. Cliff Norvell, an understudy to Bettencourt in 1930, was moved to center, where on Sunday he would go up against his old mentor, for the center of the Warriors' line, who were coached and captained by Garland Grange, was anchored by the redoubtable Larry Bettencourt; also in their backfield was Whitey Shelton.

The Warriors arrived at noon on Saturday, worked out at Hodges Field, and quartered at the Chisca Hotel. Sunday was unseasonably warm, and over 2,000 people attended the game. The Tigers took an early lead on a ten-yard touchdown pass from Seiberling to Peters, and in the second quarter, following a blocked punt by Johnny Faulkner, the ball bouncing off his chest, increased it to 13-0 when Cohen, who had shed twenty-five pounds since stepping off the train from Benoit, Mississippi, blasted into the end zone from the 5-yard line. On defense, despite Bettencourt's aggressive reactions, they were able to stop the Warriors' running game, but had trouble defending against the pass, and Peter's dropkicks were off their mark.

Garland Grange impressed with his ability to catch passes in a crowd and in the last quarter almost turned the game around. He intercepted a lateral intended for Rose and sprinted twenty yards to the end zone. The Warriors got the ball back and drove down the field on passes from Leahy to Grange until Rose made a clutch interception. Then the Tigers drove down to the 15-yard line where Peters, attempting to dropkick a field goal, was swarmed by the opposition, fumbled, and Lally of the Warriors picked up the loose ball and ran fifty yards before Rose caught him from behind. The Tigers' defense rallied, they got the ball back, and Peters punted.

But once again on passes from Leahy to Grange, the Warriors drove down the field and were at the 15-yard line, the final seconds ticking off the clock, when Faulkner tackled Leahy for a ten-yard loss and the Tigers escaped with a 13-7 victory. The Memphis backfield, regarded by local fans as one of the best in the nation, had played the entire game and was exhausted at the end, lack of reserve strength nearly causing them to lose, and their opponent on the following Sunday was the undefeated St. Louis Gunners, probably the best independent pro football team in the country.

Rose In Full Bloom

Gene Rose

The Gunners played before hometown crowds that often exceeded 10,000 and had in their backfield two flashy, broken field runners named Red Saussele and Gil Lebebvre, a tiny French American weighing only 150 pounds, who as a Cincinnati Red still holds the NFL record (set in 1933) for a punt return of 102 yards. Their line was big and had NFL experience, and they came to Memphis well prepared, having just beaten the Cleveland Bulldogs 33-0, because word had been spread by the Warriors that the Tigers this year were as good as the team of Clarence Saunders. The Gunners suited up twenty-four players.

Jess Eberdt had gotten homesick playing for the Brooklyn Dodgers and asked for his release. He wired from New York that he would be back by the end of the week. Cavette, still suffering from the shoulder injury, also returned to the Tiger lineup, and on Sunday more than 3,000 fans were in the stands. The Tigers had scant few on their bench, Goat Hale himself entering the game in the fourth quarter after Rose and Seiberling had been taken out. But they played tenaciously. Five times in the first half the Gunners drove deep into Tiger territory but scored only once. Rose halted one drive with an interception at the 10-yard line and, later in the third quarter, dashed down the sidelines all the way to the end zone, but officials ruled he had stepped out of bounds and disallowed the touchdown.

The game was roughly played, and Tigers dropped out; Cavette and Getz were already playing hurt. Still, in the final

108-Yard Booter Opposes Tigers Sunday

He's never satisfied and can always be depended on to kick about something before the game is over, is Bud Brubaker, star back of the St. Louis Gunners, professional football team.

The Gunners will fire volleys, broadsides, salvos and what have you at the Memphis Bry's Tigers at Hodges Field Sunday in what should be the grid classic of the season. Brubaker has covered 108 yards in a single boot. He was a member of Pop Warner's All-Coast team in 1931.

FIGHTING VOLS AND DUKE ARE RARIN' TO GO

Tennessee Favored to Win But Hard Battle Expected In Knoxville

KNOXVILLE, Tenn. (UP)—The Tennessee Vols will attempt to keep their undefeated record of the season unmarred this afternoon as they battle the rejuvenated Duke Blue Devils before a homecoming crowd.

Major Bob Neyland, Vol coach, will start a new backfield combination consisting of Harvey Robinson, quarterback, Feathers and Vaughn at halfback and Middleton at fullback.

The probable lineup:

Tennessee	Position	Duke
Rayburn	L. E.	James
Franklin	L. T.	Crawford
Hills	L. G.	Schno...
Maples	Center	Dunla...
Prock	R. G.	Andre...
Capt. Aixen	R. T.	Porter
Warmath	R. E.	Rossit...
Robinson	Q. B. Capt.	Masou...
Feathers	L. H.	Lan...
Vaughn	R. H.	Cro...
Middleton	F. B.	Fraht...

MRS. SOLOMON IS WINNER IN CHATTANOOGA

Memphis Woman Star Takes Title By Defeating Another Bluff Citian

CHATTANOOGA, Tenn. — Running her 40-foot putt to the cup on the seventeenth green of the Chattanooga Golf and Country Club yesterday to win the club's invitation...

BUD BRUBAKER

FIGHTING IRISH

Great Gunner Kicker

minutes they drove down the field. Hale broke through tackle for twenty-four yards to put the ball in the 15-yard line, and then Cohen made eight more yards on two line plunges. But there they stalled and the Gunners got the ball back and punted. The final score was 0-6, the Tigers recording their only loss of the season.

The *Memphis Press-Scimitar* wrote, "When the Gunners flooded the field with a profusion of subs the local cats were forced to leave the battered remnants in the game. And when the Tigers' drive did get started there was no fresh blood to steam the attack up to the touchdown point."

Here's Newest Tiger

GARLAND GRANGE

Garland Grange joins Tigers

A fan named F. C. Russell wrote into Pigue's column, "Give them two rugged ends of Tillie Voss's ability, with Cavette as a reserve; another lineman as good as Long, and two backfield reserves of even average ability, and they will go places and do things."

Management took heed to bolster the roster by sending wires out across the country, scouring the land for players, and received a response from one of the most famous names in sports. Early in the week, addressing the problem of reserve strength, the papers prophetically announced that a famous player would soon be signing.

The Tigers signed Garland Grange, younger brother of the great Red Grange, who like his older brother had played at Illinois and made the all-Big Ten team in 1928. Red Grange himself was in New York City that week to play against the Giants. From his hotel room Red spoke to reporters about the present and future state of professional football and what he said was very astute and amazingly accurate. He predicted that "the great American sport twenty years from now will be professional football played at night in huge, indoor stadiums.

"Weather has been the greatest obstacle to the professional game's progress since its beginning ten years ago." Emphasizing that most colleges were not bothered by the weather:

TICKETS ARE SOLD in advance and the game is played as scheduled, regardless of the weather – whether the fans come or not. But the big ticket sale for the professional games comes on the day of the contest. If the weather is bad, the promoters are thrown for a loss that cuts down their profits on good game days.

Commercial football is catching on amazingly. There are three reasons for this: 1) the professionals play better than the collegians, 2) it gives the chap who hasn't gone to a college a team to cheer for, and 3) the prices are within reach of the average man. The most important of those reasons is that the butchers, bricklayers, plumbers, mechanics, truck drivers and their wives get a team they can call their own. Most people haven't gone to college so why should they get all excited over a college game. But give them their Dodgers, Giants, or Bears and they're out there yelling their heads off as loudly as any alumnus cheering for Old Ruggles.

Insightful were his reasons behind the growing, however slowly, popularity of professional football, and this probably without knowledge that television would some day come into living rooms. And since forty years later, in twice the time he predicted, professional football has regularly been played at night and in huge indoor stadiums, Red Grange had true premonitions of the future.

Van Sickle Mows 'Em

CLYDE VAN SICKLE

Bry's Tiger Wingman

DUMMY MONOHAN

Tiger Lineman Clyde Van Sickle (left) and Dummy Monahan (right)

Along with Garland Grange the Tigers signed Bunny Belden, the other half of the Cardinals' "Pony Backfield," who had also become dissatisfied with Jack Chevigny, the Cardinals' new coach. Belden weighed 165 pounds and could run 100 yards in 10 seconds. He watched from the sidelines at Thursday's practice and on Friday donned a uniform. He and Rose, who had been roommates with the Cardinals, were elated over their reunion.

Friday's practice was long and hard. Hale had devised new plays to better use the new players' speed. Their opponent on Sunday was Mills Stadium, who had no starting player over 200 pounds but were fast and synchronized and dangerous on a dry field. However, by noon on Saturday rain began falling just as the Tigers were holding a light workout, and it continued to fall through Sunday.

Hodges Field became a swamp, and the stands were almost empty. During the game the ball had to be wiped off between plays. Dummy Monahan had had his picture in *The Commercial Appeal* on Saturday morning, underneath explaining how Coach

In Lineups for Pro Battle at Hodges Field This Afternoon

Tony Lawless
(H.B., Mills)

Jess Eberdt
(Center, Tigers)

"Corny" Collins
(Q.B., Mills)

Mill Stadium returns

Hale gave him hand signals telling what to do when he was on the field. He could hear neither the roar of the crowd nor the boos of the fans, and it was he who turned the game into a rout.

The Tigers played with power and scored twice on long drives before Mills Stadium mounted any offense. Then in the second quarter when the visitors drove into Tiger territory, Monahan intercepted and ran seventy-two yards for a touchdown and the rout was on, with the Tigers scoring again minutes later on a pass from Peters to Getz. Soon after the second half began, Peters kicked a forty-two-yard field goal. (The ball flinging mud as it traveled end over end through the goal posts.) And in the fourth quarter, after a Mills Stadium back had been tackled for a safety, Grange took the ball on a reverse, faked a line plunge, whirred to his left, and went like an arrow twenty-five yards to the end zone. The final score was 40-0, and Chick Harley, still coach of Mills Stadium, graciously applauded the victors.

On the following Tuesday, November 8, Franklin Delano Roosevelt was elected by a landslide to his first term of office.

Hopes of Bry's Tigers To Even Score With St. Louis Gunners

FROSTY PETERS (Q.B.)

Benny Belden (L.H.)

GENE ROSE

Tiger Hopes against the Gunners

That evening the players, including again the tall, rangy Al Culver, management, and members of the press attended a dinner at the Devoy Hotel hosted by Ed Solomon. The future was uncertain, but Soloman was reassuring and planned organized promotions to help increase attendance. Lucrative offers to relocate had come from other cities, Birmingham, Alabama, being one, but Soloman wanted the Tigers playing in Memphis, feeling that with good teams on the schedule and a fair break in the weather large crowds might still appear.

The Chickasas Buddies, a large club for boys fourteen and under that granted at reduced prices special sections to them at games and allowed them to mingle with the players at Saturday practices, was organized. And on Saturday, instead of the usual short signal drill, the players, some of them arriving early to demonstrate basic formations and kicking techniques to the Chickasas Buddies, worked out for three hours, because heavy rains had canceled previously scheduled practices during the week.

The game on Sunday was a rematch against the St. Louis Gunners, who were no longer undefeated, having lost to the powerful Portsmouth Spartans 0-12 on Wednesday night. And with deceptive spinners, cutback, and end-around runs set up by double and triple-reverses designed to get Peters and Belden and Grange into the open field, Hale planned to circumnavigate their strong line while the defense concentrated on stopping Saussele and Lefebvre. The game plan went well, and this time it was the Gunners who tried to come from behind.

In the first quarter Belden returned a punt to set up a score where Grange, on an end-around to the left developing from a fake reverse, swept into the end zone from the 2-yard line. Then early in the fourth quarter, following another punt return by Belden, Peters dropped back and hit Rose with a perfect pass and Rose, leaving a crowd behind him, dashed twenty yards for the score to make it 12-0, and it would stay that way.

Has Goods

—Press-Scimitar Photo.

Goat Hale

The Gunners' explosive offense finally broke loose, but their comeback was ruined by Saussele; had he not fumbled twice, the ending might have been different. First, Lefebvre broke loose, chased by Belden, and raced down the sidelines seventy-six yards until caught from behind by Belden. Then on the next play Saussele fumbled at the 1-yard line, and Belden recovered for the Tigers. He fumbled again in the waning minutes with the Gunners on the Tigers' 3-yard line.

So the Tigers avenged their only loss of the season, and the teams would meet again two weeks later in St. Louis, with the Gunners having supplanted the Hominey Indians as the Tigers' main rival. Hale's complex offensive plays, which the backfield talent enabled him to employ, were working well, and on defense Solly Cohen was outstanding. But they were not doing well at the gate.

Bob Pique issued a warning in the *Memphis Press-Scimitar.*

MEMPHIS FOOTBALL FANS will have to better support the Tigers or they're going to fold up like the family accordion. This comes straight from the feed box after Sunday's disappointing crowd . . . [even though] the game was one of the greatest ever played in the South . . . the fans stayed away by the thousands. About 1900 fans paid their way into the game, which left the backers of the team holding the bag to the tune of $100 or more. And they can't go on indefinitely losing money. Better support must be had by the Tigers or they'll soon kick the bucket. And that's no baloney.

Their next game was against the Milwaukee Nitehawks, and some old faces dropped from the roster as new ones appeared. Among others, Blankenbaker, Thomason, and Getz were released (Blankenbaker and Getz to return the following year) as tackle Joe Moore, who had been playing for the Gunners, switched back to the Tigers, and Norman Shelley, a broken field runner from the University of Texas, was signed from the Providence Steamrollers. And when Eberdt had left Brooklyn he brought veteran tackle Harvey Long (6', 205 pounds) with him. Long spent the 1930 and '31 seasons with the Nitehawks and now played well for the Tigers. The *Memphis Press-Scimitar* gave notice by putting his picture in Saturday's paper, looking long in the tooth, he had big ears and wore number 60, just a few hours before the Nitehawks stepped off the train.

Man of the 'Hour'

Harvey Long

The skies cleared on Sunday. Two thousand people were in the stands. Rose broke loose around right end and galloped forty-six yards to the Nitehawk 12. A penalty moved the ball to the one, and Peters skirted into the end zone. Thus, the tempo was set early. A few minutes later Belden returned a punt deep into Nitehawk territory, and Grange scored on a reverse. The reserves came off the bench, and the Tigers continued to score, at half time it was 27-0, but the first half was marred by a terrible accident. Clay Ehlers, Milwaukee's quarterback, was injured on a drive deep in Tiger territory. He got up and walked off the field, but then suddenly toppled over and was taken to the Baptist Hospital with a fractured skull.

In the second half Monahan returned another interception for a touchdown, catching the ball off his shoestrings to dash untouched fifty-two yards to the end zone. And in the fourth quarter Cohen smashed in from the one to make the final score 41-0. But all was not so sad for the Nitehawks. When their train left Memphis that night, Clay Ehlers was with them.

A fan wrote into Pigue's column,

> IF THE TIGER management, with the help of newspapers, could get out and sell 10,000 tickets at say 50 cents each for one of the games we could be assured of finishing the season with as great a sport as could be provided . . . Would certainly hate to see that great team disbanded. I have seen every Tiger game this year, and must say that football fans simply don't know what they are missing by not attending. Those boys can play the game in a manner that few college games can approach. Anyone who saw that great race between Lefebvre of Navy and Belden of St. Mary's had a slight fever from excitement.

Two games were scheduled on the following weekend. In addition to traveling to St. Louis on Sunday, the Tigers were to play the Hominey Indians on Saturday in a game that would benefit the Elks-Appeal Christmas Fund, (Ed Soloman, not so coincidentally, was the exalted ruler of the Elks) and the players worked hard in preparation. Some of them were conscripted in the late afternoons and early evenings to sell tickets at booths placed advantageously throughout the city—tickets were $1.00

Two of Gunners Who Will Shoot at Local Tigers Today

Mack Gladden (end)   George Dye (fullback)

Gunners in the game

for adults and 25 cents for children, as Hale doubled practices.
But by Friday the Indians' game was canceled because of a
scheduling problem. The Central-Tech High game had been re-
scheduled to that Saturday with both principles insisting upon
the new date and public-relations-minded Godman did not want
to interfere. The Indians were already en route to Memphis and
efforts to reach them were unsuccessful. So it was agreed that
they could stay over and play on the following week.

The Tigers, twenty men strong, left for St. Louis on Saturday
night and the next day at the Public School Stadium they played
before the largest crowd all season (nearly 10,000) without being hindered by the aches and bruises of preceding battle. The
Gunners wanted into the NFL and had added Joe Lintzenich
and Swede Johnson to strengthen their roster. Both men played
decisive roles in a scoreless tie. Lintzenich matched punts with
Peters, booming their long, arching kicks more than half the
length of the field to confine play between the 30-yard lines, and
Johnson knocked out Belden when the Tigers were threatening
in the third quarter.

Al Culver of the Tigers, having performed poorly in his first two games, was at last up to form and opened so many holes in the line, that to stop him Lintzenich began holding. The referees did not see it, or would not call it, so Lintzenich continued until Culver smacked him in the eye. The Tigers started to move downfield, slashing their runners through the line, and might have scored had not Belden, just after catching a pass from Peters, been knocked out. Without him, the drive fizzled. But that was not the only chance they had for victory. Peters missed on five field goal attempts. When the gun ended the game, the score remained 0-0. So this year they split their games against the Gunners, not faring as well on the following season.

Culver had replaced Van Sickle, who pulled a ligament and then came down with the flu. But the rest of the team was healthy and helped man ticket booths for the Elks-Appeal Christmas Fund and were active in other community affairs as well. Peters and Faulkner spoke at an Exchange Club luncheon, and Grange and McMullen appeared before the Kiwanis. Then on Friday, Peters, Grange, and McMullen spoke at the Tech High assembly.

But, and this being in no way related to football and the Tigers, there was a greater presence in town during the week. The youngest daughter of the great Russian writer Leo Tolstoy, Countess Alexandra Tolstoy, was staying at the Tennessee Hotel and on Friday and Saturday nights delivered lectures at the Goodwyn Institute. Having spent time in a Russian prison, the countess told reporters that American women to her looked like children, because they have known so little.

At the end of this week, the Tigers grabbed headlines in the sports sections with the announcement (which as a rumor the week before had been denied by Godman: "We are well fixed for football players now!" he had said) that the great Ernie Nevers would be joining their backfield to play against the Chicago Cardinals. Godman claimed they could not afford him; the team was in the red, and the games were not drawing well; but Soloman had agreed to guarantee both his expenses and salary. The next game, as previously promised, was against the Hominey Indians.

The Indians had their usual strange and colorful array. Six different tribes, Cherokee, Creek, Osage, Seneca, Sioux, and

Seminole, were represented on their roster. Their players going by such tribal aliases as Red Tomahawk, One Feather, Spotted Horn, and Brave Thunder, including Alex "Two Gun" Floyd, a running back and the younger half-brother of Pretty Boy Floyd, who was still out on the loose being sought for bank robbery and kidnapping. There was also Chief Fixico, well known to Memphis fans because the year before he had lost his temper and, wildly swinging both arms, challenged every Tiger on the field to fight.

On Sunday December 4 a cloud cover held warm temperatures over the region, 2,000 people were in the stands, and the Indians played like savages. No longer considering them keen opposition, the Tigers used mostly reserves along with new men. Chang Artman (6' 4", 230 pounds), a tackle from Stanford and the New York Giants, and end Kermit Schmidt (6', 200 pounds) from Cal Poly were added to the roster. Goat Hale played the entire game without helmet or shoulder pads.

In the first quarter after an exchange of punts, Rose dropped back and rifled the ball to Cavette for a touchdown. The extra point was blocked, and a few minutes later Hale, fielding a punt, tried to lateral to Rose, but an Indian pounced on the ball. Then Fixico broke loose. Grabbed and spun at the line, he remained on his feet to run pigeon-toed down the sidelines, the only Tiger between him and the goal knocked down, and loped unmolested into the end zone. The extra point was good, and the Indians took a 7-6 lead. But they could not hold onto it.

In the second quarter Cavette blocked a punt, and the Indians were penalized on the next play for gang tackling, which moved the ball to their 12-yard line where Hale swept

On Local Grid Sunday

SOLLY COHEN

Solly Cohen

around right end for a touchdown. For the rest of the afternoon Peters's long punts bottled them up, and the Tigers scored again in the fourth quarter on a disputed play. When an Indian punt went up in the air and came down backwards, an Indian caught it, but Cohen grabbed the ball and, with the Indian around his neck, tumbled into the end zone. The Indians aggressively protested, claiming that Cohen had never had possession. But officials let the play stand, and the final score was 20-7.

That evening Ernie Nevers boarded a train in San Francisco traveling with the Alabama football team, which was returning from a game against St. Mary's. On Wednesday morning, December 7, he stepped off a Rock Island Pullman at Grand Central Station. There to greet him were a swarm of reporters and former teammates Belden and Rose. Dressed nicely in a suit and tie and hungry for breakfast, Nevers took time to predict an Irish victory in the upcoming Notre Dame-South Cal clash (Southern Cal won 13-7) and told reporters that after Sunday's game he would probably fly back to Palo Alto, where he had just spent the season as an assistant coach at Stanford, because Pop Warner had resigned as head coach, and he was anxious about the possibility that the job might be his.

Blond Bear Greeted by Ex-Cardinals

Nevers arrives in Memphis

That night he practiced with the Tigers at Hodges Field. Hale inserted a few of Pop Warner's double-wing formations into the offense, and at Thursday's practice Belden quarterbacked and Nevers was fullback. On Friday they concentrated on defense: Nevers backed up the line and would do all the punting.

Across the state in Knoxville that night, history was made: thirteen members withdrew from the old and unwieldy Southern Conference to form a new compact league patterned after the Big Ten. The name of the new league was The Southeastern Conference.

Tickets to the Cardinals' game sold so well that management dispensed with the free section for the Chickasas Buddies and put those seats up for sale. The Cardinals arrived Saturday evening and were ruled slight favorites despite their 2-6-2 record. The kickoff was scheduled for 2:30 on the following afternoon, but the weather was causing more trouble.

Memphis was hit by an ice storm late Friday night, (the Tigers had practiced at Beauregard Field on Saturday to not ruin the turf at Hodges) and then early Sunday morning it began to rain. At noon, Treadwell and Godman met with Dr. David Jones of the Cardinals and postponed the game until Tuesday night. The Boston Braves were already in town, their game against the Gunners in St. Louis canceled by snow, and were quartered with the Cardinals at the Chisca Hotel.

Rain continued to fall, and the temperature dropped. A flu epidemic swept through the city. Team officials, not wanting to jeopardize anyone's health, postponed the game again late Tuesday afternoon, this time for good, and the Cardinals returned to Chicago. Tickets would be honored against the Braves on Sunday, no new ones were printed, and Stanford University extended Nevers's leave of absence. The Tigers needed a large crowd. They were $5,000 in debt, but this was small change compared to the Braves.

At a time when the average salary in the NFL was less than $100 a game; great players like Red Grange and the Giants' Chris Cagle were paid $500, the Bears' Bronko Nagurski made $300; the Boston Braves had one of the highest payrolls in the league. Nineteen thirty-two was their first year, and they started the season with four owners. Despite relative success on

ORAN PAPE

This stellar ex-Iowa star plays quarterback for the Boston Braves, and will be in the Beantown lineup against the Memphis Bry's Tigers Sunday at Hodges Field. He was All-America for two years, and once ran the 100 in 9:07 to defeat Eddie Tolan, Olympic 100 and 200 champion. He is said to be the fastest man in the National Pro League.

Oran Pape of the Braves

the field, tying the eventual champion Chicago Bears and finishing in fourth place with a 4-4-2 record, they lost $46,000, so three of the original owners washed their hands of pro football. But the one who remained, George Preston Marshall, was determined to hang on.

They came to Memphis with only fifteen players. Missing from their roster were star halfbacks Cliff Battles (6' 1", 194 pounds) and Ernie Pinckert (6', 197 pounds), an all-American at Southern Cal in '31. Battles, who had finished the season with 650 yards rushing, second only to Dutch Clark of the Portsmouth Spartan, was in Charleston, West Virginia, taking exams for a Rhodes Scholarship. But they still had plenty of talent. Their quarterback, Oren Pape, having been timed in the 100-yard dash at 9.7 seconds, was probably the fastest man in the NFL and had once outrun 1932 Olympic gold medalist Eddie Tolan. The fullback was big Jim Musick, a teammate of Pinckert's at Southern Cal, and only Nagurski was considered better at that position. And their line was big and strong with two giant tackles: Hugh Rhea (6' 3", 225 pounds) and all-pro Turk Edwards (6' 2", 258 pounds). Rhea was an Olympic shot putter, and Edwards was their coach on the road. One of their reserves was former Tiger Cowboy Woodruff.

Two inches of snow fell on Friday as temperatures dropped to twelve degrees. On Saturday a city grader moved into Hodges Field and sliced off snow and ice, piling it into banks outside the playing field. Then on Sunday December 18 a sweeper was brought in to clear off the remainder, but it adhered to the frozen surface, and under a blue sky the field had turned white.

The yard lines and boundaries were marked with coal dust, and it was so cold that the players' frozen breath could be seen from a distance. Only about 750 fans attended, several of them huddling around a fire at one end of the field. The field judge, Zach Curlin, wore earmuffs.

Bob Pigue called it "Ice Hockey." Offense was rendered impossible. In the second quarter Nevers made the longest gain of the day when he faked a punt and sprinted twenty-seven yards only to have the ball slip out of his hands when tackled.

Turk Edwards of the Braves

The men slipped and skidded. Most of the plays went pell-mell and ended in tumbled heaps, and the game became a punting duel between Nevers and Red Rust of Boston and ended in a scoreless tie. Neither team was satisfied, and they agreed to play again on Christmas Day. Nevers, who carried the ball on almost every play, boarded a train and returned to California. (At Stanford he would not become the head coach.)

Grange and Van Sickle left town and were replaced in the starting lineup by Schmidt and Norvell. Cold, wet weather continued, and several Braves came down with the flu. In desperate need of reserve strength, the Braves signed a back from Harvard named Johnny Crickard on Friday. By then the sky had cleared, and Hodges Field was beginning to dry. Hale told the press that the Tigers' best chance for victory would be "to take to the air." The Braves were favored by two touchdowns because of the size and strength of their line.

On Sunday the sun raked across Hodges Field on a beautiful Christmas Day. On defense the Tigers were impenetrable up the middle, so Boston ran their backs around the ends, and near the end of the first half drove down to the 1-yard line where Norvell broke through the line and tackled Pape for a five-yard loss. The Braves smothered the Tigers' offense, but Peters's long

The Athleticism of Ernie Nevers

punts kept them out of trouble for the rest of the afternoon, and the game ended in another scoreless tie.

Fewer people had been in the stands than were there the week before. Pigue wrote that the crowd "wouldn't have filled a phone booth," and there was no money to meet Boston's guarantee. When George Treadwell went to the Chisca Hotel to tell this to the Braves, one of the players stood up and made threats. Somehow, later, and not because of the threats, the money was paid. But when Treadwell sent Frosty Peters to Nashville to try and arrange a game with the Bears, Halas was not interested.

Boston traveled on to Nashville where on the following day before another very small crowd they were trounced by the Chicago Bears at Dudley Field. During the game some of the fans amused themselves by setting off fireworks. However, the Braves were destined for greater things. The next year Marshall renamed them the Redskins, hired several Indian players and an Indian head coach, Lone Star Dietz, and on opening day of

Sought to Play Here

PEPPER MARTIN

Here's Pepper Martin, St. Louis here next Sunday. Pepper would Cardinal outfielder, who is playing be a big drawing card here, and pro football in Oklahoma, and all possible efforts will be made whose team is being sought to play to get him.

Pepper Martin

the new season the entire squad, made up with war paint and wearing feathered headdresses, posed for a team picture. The Indian players were used only as a promotional ploy and were not very good, but behind the blocking of Edwards and Jack Riley, Musick and Battles lead the NFL in rushing. The team remained in Boston only a few more years; Marshall became dissatisfied there and moved them to Washington, DC, where he owned a chain of laundries. And thus it was, that's how the Boston Braves, twice stalemated by the Memphis Tigers, became the Washington Redskins.

Peters, now acting as a front office man, was unable to bring the Bears, but a few days later he scheduled a game for New

Year's Day against the Oklahoma Chiefs who had in their back-field the hero of the 1931 World Series, Pepper Martin of the St. Louis Cardinals. Several familiar Indian names were also on their roster, along with former Tiger and former Hominey Indian Whitey Shelton, and though the press made it clear that they were not the Hominey Indians, some fans still mistakenly thought they were.

When they arrived at Union Station on Saturday, reporters gathered around Pepper Martin as he stepped off the train. Martin, dressed in a suit, predicted a National League Pennant for the St. Louis Cardinals in '33, then went with his team to spend New Year's Eve at the Chisca Hotel. The next day he would prove to be almost as good at football as he was at baseball.

New Year's Day came sunny, but less than 500 people were in the stands. The Tigers had signed Turk Edwards to play on the line and took a 13-0 lead in the second quarter. But the Chiefs came back. They had the ball deep in their own terri-tory when Martin swept around left end, found an opening that he hustled through, then reversed his field and galloped like a pony seventy-five yards to the end zone. The Tigers scored again in the third quarter on a long pass from Peters to Faulkner and seemed on a roll. But in the fourth quarter when Pepper Mar-tin reentered the game, he caught a pass off his shoestrings, eluded two tacklers, and gamboled twenty-five yards to the end zone to make the final score 19-13.

Both teams crossed the Mississippi River to play again on the following evening in Blytheville, Arkansas. Eberdt had ar-ranged the game, but too few people showed up, and it was canceled. The season was over. Excellence on the field had pro-duced a 7-1-3 record, one of the best of the Tiger teams, which had thus far accumulated a record of 39-12-5—very good by any standards; but at the gate, it had been the most disastrous year yet.

The city seemed to have lost interest in its professional foot-ball team, especially in the last few games, and it was now less certain than ever that they would carry on. However, change was in the air. In the North, pro football was getting stronger. Frosty Peters felt this and, inspired by victories of the season just past, remained in Memphis to try again.

ALMOST BUSTED

*I*N THE EARLY SPRING and summer of 1933 George Halas
and George Preston Marshall lead the way for much-need-
ed innovations in the professional game to create wide-open
play that would produce more field goals, more passing, and
more points. At the end of its July meeting the NFL adopted
three significant rules changes: 1) the goal posts were moved
from the back of the end zone to the goal line (this was reversed
again in 1974); 2) passing became permitted anywhere behind
the line of scrimmage (instead of from at least five yards back);
and 3) the ball would be moved ten yards in from the sidelines
on any play ending within five yards of the sidelines. The ball

George Halas   *George Preston Marshall*

itself, originally a fat inflated bladder, was narrowed and conformed, at last reaching its present shape, and ending forever the days of the dropkick.

Stirred by the dynamic change, Godman took control and made moves that would guarantee Memphis its place in professional football a little while longer. In early August the *Memphis Press-Scimitar* reported that Clarence Saunders was again considering backing the Tigers and wanted Bucky Moore as a player-coach. Nothing came of that, but a month later when Godman met with Frosty Peters, things began to happen.

In an office in the Sterick Building they mapped out strategy: Peters would coach and manage, and Godman would manage and advise. The team would operate on a cooperative basis as it did in '31 with profit from the gate evenly shared. They offered season tickets priced at $10 for a book of ten, and organized another club for boys twelve and under; calling it the Tiger Cubs, on its first day of registration nearly 100 boys gathered with their parents in the lobby of the Chisca Hotel to join.

Godman was approached by S. H. Jones from Oklahoma, the former manager of the Hominey Indians, about joining a proposed Southwestern Professional Football league. He declined, finding the idea too unlikely, but agreed to the possibility of games against would-be participants. When Peters was sent to Chicago on Friday September 15, workouts had already started at Hodges Field. The intense heat of the summer lingered, and there was promise in some of the men. But half the players were new, and

Tigers open new season with Frosty Peters

the character of the Tigers took on a different coloration: in 1933 they lost as much as they won.

Peters saw the Bears play the Notre Dame All-Stars at Soldier Field on Saturday, wired Godman that he expected to sign four or five good players, and on Sunday watched the Cardinals against a team from Aurora, Illinois, then started back to Memphis, stopping in Urbana along the way for a visit with his old coach and mentor Bob Zuppke, who showed him some new trick plays. McMullen coached in Peters' absence, and more veterans returned.

Harvey Long, who had been working out with the Pittsburgh Pirates of the NFL, and Gerald Seiberling arrived on the following Wednesday. Fred Getz and Vic Saufley, a 205-pound end from SMU recommended by Ernie Nevers, came on Thursday. On Friday, September 22, practice became twice a day. Under the arc lights with 200 fans watching, Jess Eberdt appeared and immediately dislodged Marty McManus from the starting job at center. Eberdt was coaching at the high school in Hot Springs, Arkansas, and arranged to have the weekends off. Bobby Rogers, a 215-pound back released from the Cardinals, joined on Saturday, and S. T. Reese from Tupelo, a cousin of Gil Reese and whose brief career as an NFL player had ended with a back injury, was hired as trainer.

Fullback Punch McDaniels returned on the following Tuesday, and on Wednesday night during the high school jamboree at Hodges Field the Tigers demonstrated the single and double-wing and short punt formations. Two veteran NFL backs, Ed Storm (6' 1", 195 pounds) and Swede Ellstrom (6' 1", 203 pounds) were signed the next day. The first game of the season was scheduled for Sunday October 1 against the Cincinnati Reds, the newest entry in the NFL, and on Friday Indian Fait Elkins showed up with their offensive plays.

Elkins, an Olympian once through the possible successor to Jim Thorpe, had left the Reds enraged after a misunderstanding with head coach Al Jolly. In an exhibition game the week before, he had thrown a touchdown pass, but not to the intended receiver, and Jolly, unhappy over the play-call transgression, harshly expressed his disapproval. The conflict heated, and Elkins bolted. So on Saturday morning the Tigers practiced defense against

Fait Elkins

Cincinnati plays described by Elkins. This may have helped, but not on offense where the team lacked almost any coordination.

On Sunday morning in *The Commercial Appeal* another changing aspect of professional football was observed by Early Maxwell. "Pro football," he wrote, "is progressing to the point where the player has to establish himself in the pro game, no matter what previous college fame he has gained, before he is a steady drawing card at the gate."

That afternoon before 3,000 fans, the punchless Tigers went scoreless. Cincinnati threatened throughout the first half but managed only a field goal; Earl Pate of the Tigers intercepted to stop one drive just as the half was ending, but in the second half they wore down the Tigers' defense and twice scored on long drives for a 0-17 shutout. Getz, his temper again flaring, was ejected for rough play near the end. If the city did not support a winner, then, certainly, it would not support a loser. Those watching closely could feel as if the death bell of a once-magnificent football team had made its first loud knell.

Afterward, Getz was again told to control his temper, and Bobby Rogers, a disappointment, was cut from the squad. The Reds made offers to Peters, Norvell, and McMullen, but each was turned down. Peters, also rejecting an offer to play the next game in Birmingham, practiced the team on Monday, usually the one day off during the week, and three times on Tuesday, telling reporters that they wanted "to redeem themselves before the Memphis fans for the Cincinnati defeat before taking to the road." But despite this commitment, things got worse before they got better. On Sunday they played the Oklahoma Chiefs, minus Pepper Martin. Only 710 people paid their way into the game, and the Tigers were shutout again.

The Chiefs were small but had a well-balanced attack, (six of their players had played together on an undefeated University of Oklahoma City team in 1931) and they seized upon the Tigers' weak pass defense to score twice through the air. The Tigers mustered some offense in the second half, but an alert Chief defense, intercepting three times, stopped them whenever they approached the goal line. Though still confused by some fans with the Hominey Indians, the Chiefs played much smarter than the Indians had ever played.

The future looked dismal for the Tigers. Debts mounted, and it was rumored they would either disband or move to Birmingham. In *The Commercial Appeal* on Wednesday Bob Pigue suggested, "Reduce the admission prices . . . the increase in fans will net more money at the gate even tho they pay less to get in. It is better to play before 2,000 fans at 50 cents per head than 1,000 fans at $1 per head."

The backfield, which had been so good the year before, was a keen disappointment, and Peters, who had injured his shoulder, sent off telegrams in search of quality backs. The only response came from Solly Cohen, and when he arrived on Thursday he was again overweight. However, Godman felt a possible windfall and moved to take advantage. The World Series had just ended, and the hero of the game was a Memphian named Bill Terry.

Bill Terry

Terry, a remarkable baseball player—the last American Leaguer to break .400 in batting—had just led the New York Giants to victory over the Washington Senators in five games. Left-handed, born in Atlanta, his family had moved to Memphis after the turn of the century. He started playing professional baseball in his teens, pitching for Shreveport in the Texas League, and was such a fine pinch-hitter that the major leagues soon came bidding. But the price asked by Shreveport was too high, so Terry quit on his own and returned to Memphis, married, and worked for Standard Oil operating a chain of gas stations, playing on the company baseball team.

As they passed through town on their way to training camp in San Antonio, the Giants signed him to play first base in the spring of 1922. He started off slowly, batting .143 his first season in the majors, but after that his average soared. Beginning in 1927, he drove in 100 runs for six consecutive seasons and batted .372 in '29 and .401 in '30. Already a national figure, the Giants appointed him manager in 1932 to succeed an ailing John McGraw. Returning home after his team's great victory, Bill first stopped in Chicago to see the World's Fair.

On Saturday morning, October 14, over 100,000 people lined Main Street as Terry (6' 1", blue-eyed, and thirty-five years old) was paraded to the courthouse steps where Mayor Watkins Overton ceremoniously welcomed him back. A few blocks south at Grand Central Station the Charlotte Bantams from North Carolina arrived hardly noticed.

Godman made as much of the situation as he could, proclaiming the next day "Bill Terry Day" at Hodges Field and having the loud speaker system set up for him to address the crowd. Along with Terry, 2,000 noisy fans showed up, and the Tigers played much better. The Bantam's roster was filled with former collegiate stars from the Carolinas, and they played a spirited game. Late in the first quarter Cavette intercepted deep in Charlotte territory, and two plays later Storm ran into the end zone for the Tigers' first points of the season. But the Bantams came back on a thirty-four-yard touchdown pass from Earl Dunlop to Johnny Branch, then kicked a field goal to lead 10-7 at halftime. At this point, had the Tigers folded, it may have meant the end for Peters. But in the second half they came out and dazzled the crowd.

Running behind good interference, Pate ripped off long gains and took a lateral and breezed around right end for a touchdown. Charlotte fought back with the broken field running of Johnny Branch, but in the fourth quarter Ellstrom faked a reverse and broke free

Star Line Plunger of Tigers

Marvin Ellstrom (fb.)

Fullback Marvin Ellstrom

through the center of the line to dash thirty-five yards to the end zone and put the game almost out of reach. The knockout blow came in the waning minutes when Ellstrom heaved a long touchdown pass to Saufley, and the Tigers won 27-10.

Maxwell called the game "the most spectacular battle waged here since 1930 when the Portsmouth Spartans of the National League were beaten." The offense had at last congealed, and the season looked more interesting. But on or off the field, no one was really satisfied.

In *The Commercial Appeal,* in an article that was written on Saturday but printed on Monday, Herbert Caldwell posed a question and provided an answer:

WHAT'S THE MATTER with the local professional team? [No] scoring threat! A 'scoring threat' on a football team is always an inspiration to his teammates to keep battling with the hope and belief that sooner or later the 'threat' will break loose. The Tigers this season are just plugging along. There is no real scoring threat. Until the Tigers acquire a scoring threat they will continue to be just a football team with little lure for the public.

And he prophetically reminded readers, "Bucky Moore was a scoring threat. He was not only the best gate attraction on the team, but kept the team inspired."

This situation was remedied with the signing of Red Saussele, a terror the year before with the St. Louis Gunners, from the Chicago Bears. He was with them on Saturday when they departed from Grand Central Station to play the Gunners in St. Louis and with him in the backfield the Tigers continued to play well. Fait Elkins, another disappointment, was released, and on the following Tuesday, after they had returned from St. Louis, Bucky Moore returned, and Punch McDaniels was released. Moore had been playing in the NFL for the Pittsburgh Pirates (later renamed the Steelers) but had gotten homesick. He and Saussele (6', 185 pounds) were almost exactly the same size, and together they gave Memphis one of the best backfield tandems in football.

The game in St. Louis was broadcast back to Memphis over the radio. The Gunners prepared for a close game, and

Returns to Tiger Lineup Today

Bucky Moore
One of the most outstanding ball carriers southern football has ever known will parade at Hodges Field again today when the Memphis Tigers' professional eleven meets the Chicago Shamrocks. He is Bucky Moore, popular figure with fans here, who will start at a halfback post for the local team.

Bucky Moore returns to the lineup

suffering, too, because of it, by placing the goal posts back ten yards. The Tigers recovered a fumble on the opening kickoff and marched down the field with clockwork precision. Storm passed to Saussele and then to Joe Gee to put the ball at the one-yard line where Ellstrom crashed over. Then Saussele caught a long pass, broke loose for a touchdown, and the lead at halftime was 13-0. But they ran out of steam in the second half, and the game turned around. The Gunners tied it up and would have won had Spudich not missed an extra point. Perhaps justifiably, the Tigers complained about the goal posts, claiming they had deliberately been placed back to thwart any field goal attempts by Peters.

The following Sunday, October 29, at Hodges Field was "Bucky Moore Day," his mother in attendance, and the Tigers evened their record to 2-2-1 with a victory over the Chicago Shamrocks. Peters had revamped the offense to take advantage of the speed of Moore and Saussele and the throwing arms of Ellstrom and Storm. The day was warm, about 80 degrees, and over 2,000 fans attended. The game was called by three officials instead of four, consistent with new NFL rules attempting to save time and better the officiating.

An alert Shamrock defense shutout the Tigers in the first half, successfully keying on Moore and repeatedly stopping drives that penetrated to the shadows of their goal posts. But the heat, an old Tiger ally, began to take its toll, and in the second half the Tigers were unstoppable. Moore scored on a pass from Storm, then minutes later they drove back down the field to within inches of the goal line, but Ellstrom fumbled. The Shamrocks punted and, catching the ball, back down the field came the Tigers. Saussele made long gains around the ends (chasing after him on one play a big Shamrock lineman was knocked out when he crashed into the stands and, resuming play a few minutes later, was given a standing ovation) and dashed into the end zone on a cut up the middle. They continued to score in the fourth quarter, two touchdowns and a safety, but the Shamrocks avoided a shutout with a long, desperate pass from midfield, and the final score was 30-7.

Moore had had a good game, but Saussele had been even better, and on the following Friday evening they were interviewed over the radio by Maxwell and each gave a different opinion about football matters. Saussele said that Ernie Nevers was the greatest back he had ever played against, while Moore picked Red Grange. That two gifted backs like Moore and Saussele were playing in the backfield was the highlight of the season. On the field the Tigers had turned things around, and all along the press had supported them and would continue to do so.

In his column a week later, right before they were about to leave on a road trip, Pigue gave notice to Peters's brilliance: "Right here in Memphis is a dropkicker who holds a flock of world records. His name is Frosty Peters. Peters was playing with Montana State against Billings Poly one afternoon and dropkicked 17 field goals . . . (his) toe is still educated, and any time he gets a chance he can bust the oval thru the bars." But Peters had not played much since injuring his shoulder early in the season, and over the next month the Tigers, though still fighting, were devastated by three straight losses.

Obscurity threatened, but Godman kept the team from dying. The next game was to have been played against the Tulsa Oilers, a recent victor over the Fort Sill Army team, which had previously tied the Oklahoma Chiefs, but problems developed, a road trip to North Carolina was planned, and it was three weeks before the Tigers again played at home.

On Friday November 3 S. H. Jones notified Godman that several of his best players would not make the trip, and Godman became angry. "If we brought the Tulsa team here under conditions forced upon us it would hurt the standing of the Tigers with the Memphis public." He told the press and sent off an ineffectual letter to Joe Carr of the NFL asking that league to boycott the Oilers.

But he was receptive when Jones again proposed a southern football league. A league seemed like it might be the key to success for pro football in the South by providing better financial backing to teams and giving them a definite schedule at the start of the season. It would also create rivalries to make the games more meaningful and zealously contested. In the North the NFL was a working example of what a league could do.

Tickets already sold to the Oilers' game were refunded or exchanged for a later game against the Gunners, and on Friday morning, November 10, the Tigers boarded a bus for North Carolina. Bucky Moore was ill and remained in Memphis. Solly Cohen, never performing as well as he had in '32, quit the team.

Nineteen players made the trip. They spent the night in Chattanooga and reached Charlotte late Saturday afternoon. On Sunday before 4,000 people at Robbie Stadium, the largest crowd to ever see a Bantam game, the Tigers lost for the first time to a team from the Deep South, an ailing Peters scoring their only points on a field goal. They limped home with injuries, stopping in Knoxville on Monday without bothering to journey on to Chattanooga where a game had been hastily scheduled against a newly organized team called the Lookouts (Peters did not want to risk any more injuries, and there was not much interest there anyway) and arrived back in Memphis on Tuesday night weary from the road.

In the midst of their demise, plans for a league were forming. Maxwell expounded on it in *The Commercial Appeal,* giving it his own vision and probably the name, when he wrote,

> THE PLAN FOR an American League in professional football is the only real hope for the sport in Memphis next year. A strong league of existing clubs, all with the prospect of someday developing into real major league caliber, can be developed. The St. Louis Gunners, Chicago Shamrocks, Wisconsin Black Hawks, Memphis Tigers, Detroit Indians, and Oklahoma Chiefs have all put up credible games against National League opposition. Personally I believe the Gunners and the Tigers game at Hodges Field Sunday gives every indication of proving as good as any in the country for the day's schedule.

Unlike the Tigers, the Gunners were a team on the rise. Strengthening an already good roster with players such as Walt Keisling, a giant 6' 3", 250-pound Tackle, whom Nevers called the best in the game, and adding the passing combination of former Southern Cal quarterback Don Moses to lanky end Charlie Malone, they demolished opponents by scores of 61-0. A few days before coming to Memphis they beat the Brooklyn Dodgers 21-2 before 6,000 hometown fans and offered the Tigers, still respected in football circles, $2,000 to transfer their game to St. Louis where they could draw a much larger crowd. But Godman, bent on future possibilities or maybe just not willing to have his team stay out on the road for three straight weeks since on the following Sunday they would play in Oklahoma City, remained loyal to Memphis fans, a small, diminishing portion of the population, and turned down the offer. The press applauded, citing it as further evidence of the faith the team was trying to keep with the public.

The Tigers were now the underdogs, and Pigue, trying to build up the gate by trumpeting the ferocious play of Gunner fullback Swede Johnson, made it look even bleaker. "Johnson was a pain in the neck to the Tiger line in St. Louis," he wrote.

Backs of St. Louis Gunners Memphis Tigers Must Stop

John Breidenstein   Dick Frahm   Joe Spudich   Swede Johnson

St. Louis Gunner backfield

"[He] likes to plunge at the hardest tackler on the enemy side. The Swede takes the pass from center fifteen yards behind the line of scrimmage and when he hits the line he is going full speed. [He] broke through the Oklahoma Chief line this season; and, finding no tacklers in his path to hit, turned around and ran through the line again."

But on Sunday the Tigers had unflinching determination, and the Gunners had to fight hard, using every weapon they had, for a victory. Soon after the opening kickoff, Ed Storm kicked a field goal for the Tigers, and they held the lead until the third quarter. The visitors amassed an astounding 472 yards from scrimmage, making twenty first downs, but the game was not decided until the final minutes.

All afternoon the Gunners moved up and down the field. When Johnson was stopped, Moses would throw to Malone. The Tigers would bend but not break and frustrated the Gunners near the goal line. Three times in the second half they stopped them inside the 10-yard line. Then the Tigers mounted a long drive in the third quarter, but failed to score, and late in the fourth quarter, deep in their own territory, Johnson intercepted and scored three plays later on an end sweep. They lost by the same score as the week before in North Carolina, 3-13.

The Gunners were offered a rematch, but their manager turned it down. "Too tough!" was his reply. And on the following week the Tigers loaded into autos and drove across Arkansas into Oklahoma, entering the rising plateau of the Great Plains, where at the Texas League ballpark in Oklahoma City they played the Chiefs before a paucity of fans.

Perhaps more interesting things took place in Memphis during the week. Dizzy Dean and his wife spent Monday night at the Chisca Hotel. The next morning their picture was taken in the restaurant smiling as they ate breakfast. And Julius Goldsmith died, the department store he founded still bearing his name. Family, friends, and associates placed a full-page tribute to his life and achievements in *The Commercial Appeal* on Saturday November 25. In Oklahoma the Chiefs used a deceptive assortment of reverses and laterals to shatter the Tigers' defense, scoring twice in the second quarter. The Tigers returned home with a 7-20 defeat and a record that had fallen to 2-5-1.

The ax fell on some of the players. "The Tigers will be entirely rebuilt within the next few days and we will not lose another game," Peters told the press. Harvey Long, Earl Pate, Joe Gee, and a reserve lineman named Ted Illness were cut to make room for new signees. Ben Fuller, a 195-pound guard from Tennessee, whom Bob Neyland said was one of the best to ever play on the Vol line, was added to the roster along with two men from Georgia, 210-pound fullback Chuck Bird and 240-pound tackle Skinny Davis, and a quarterback from NYU named Jackie Grossman. Godman declared, "We will place the strongest array of the season on the field."

But only forty-eight people paid to see them play on Saturday, and this with general admission only 85 cents. In contrast, high school games attracted large, overflowing crowds to Hodges Field. On Friday December 1 after the Tech-Central game the night before, Pigue was moved to write, "There is no place in Memphis suitable for football crowds. Yesterday at Hodges Field many hundred fans were forced to stand. A stadium is badly needed here."

The Tigers were now dangling on the edge of public notice, but still played good football and beat the punchless Atlanta Crackers 48-0 as Saussele rushed for three touchdowns. The last touchdown of the day was made by Norvell, the first of his career, when he took a lateral after an interception and ran it in. But there was not enough money to pay the officials, the police, the park rent, nor the visiting team.

Sausselle and Storm

Like a failing Broadway show that had once had great notice and was finishing its run in an obscure, out-of-town theatre, the Tigers played in Jackson, Tennessee, the next day against an old adversary they had not played in years, the West Tennessee All-Stars, who looked like a discarded image of the Tigers since most of the men who had been released had gone to Jackson and found a haven on the All-Stars' squad. Even their coach, Tiny Knee, was a former Tiger; and they played with a vengeance, scoring the first points when Gerald Seiberling kicked a field goal in the second quarter. But the Tigers came alive in the second half. Saussele broke loose on long runs, and they drove deep into All-Star territory. Finally, near the end, Bird crashed over for a 6-3 victory.

Then it appeared that the season might have a bright, shining ending, for a game against the Tennessee seniors was

Tennessee Vol Beattie Feathers

proposed, and, if so, Beattie Feathers would be on the Vol roster. Feathers was a fast, slashing halfback who had stepped out of the long shadow cast by the great Gene McEver (they had also been teammates at Tennessee High in Bristol) and scorched gridirons across the South with sensational running. He electrified the public, scoring thirty-three touchdowns in three years to help lead Tennessee to two undefeated seasons. The Vols had slumped in '33, losing twice before December, but Feathers was still brilliant on the field. Their last game of the season was on Saturday December 9 against LSU in Baton Rouge. Then it was hoped and thought that some of them might play the Tigers at Hodges Field on Sunday December 17. The seniors were eager for it since it would put them up against seasoned professionals. And so were the fans in Memphis.

One of Maxwell's readers wrote, "Hope you will see fit to pull for the proposed game between the Tennessee seniors and the Memphis Tigers. The average fan in this territory cannot afford to go to Knoxville for the Tennessee games, consequently only a few have seen Feathers and the galaxy of Vol Stars. The fans would appreciate a chance to see them in action against the Tigers."

Maxwell replied in his column,

IT'S MY OPINION Feathers and the other Tennessee stars against the Tigers will make the best football attraction Memphis has ever seen. Clarence Saunders sent me to Chicago to close the contract that brought Red Grange and his Chicago

Tigers Who Make Local Debut

SKINNY DAVIS, TACKLE
(Georgia)

CHUCK BIRD, FULLBACK
(Georgia)

Memphis Tigers in Second Game With West Tennessee Stars

Local Professional Team To Try for Second Victory
Over Foes This Afternoon at Hodges Field

New Tigers Davis and Bird

Bears here in 1929. I consider Feathers playing here even a stronger presentation, mainly because he would be at the peak of his playing form, while Grange had been 'carrying the mail' quite a number of years when he played here. Feathers is a better all-around back than Grange.

The seniors on the Tennessee football team, before they even traveled to Baton Rouge, met and unanimously voted to play the Tigers. But assistant coach Paul Parker spoke against it, warning that they could lose eligibility for further participation in intercollegiate athletics. The game was to benefit the Elks-Appeal Christmas Fund, and tickets were priced at $1.00. A Sears executive immediately applied for a hundred. The Tennessee players were to receive nothing over expenses.

Meanwhile, a rematch against the West Tennessee All-Stars had been scheduled, receiving such little coverage in the papers that the public was hardly aware of it. Ed Faulkner, who had failed to show up for the last two games, was released, and a 225-pound tackle named Marvin Moore was signed. The All-Stars added Goat Hale's younger brother Marion to their roster.

The game was played on Sunday December 10 and this time the Tigers won easily. Saussele caught an interception and weaved through the opposition fifty-five yards to the end zone. Storm passed for three touchdowns and kicked all the extra points. The final score was 35-0, and the Tigers evened their record to 5-5-1. Attendance had again been very small, but the next week's game appeared to be a sellout. It was announced that Red Cagle would be playing for the Tigers, and there was talk of installing more seats.

On Monday Maxwell received a telegram from the UT seniors confirming the game, and it was reported that they would strengthen their squad with former Vols. But on Tuesday UT chairman Nathan Dougherty announced that the seniors would not be allowed to play. "This game is scheduled in the midst of examinations and additional absences will jeopardize their [academic] standing," he said. Adding, "The game as proposed will professionalize all participants. Some of the seniors are eligible for further participation in intercollegiate activities at the university."

Edward Crump, now a United States congressman and a member of the UT Board of Trustees, made a last-minute attempt to alter the Administrative Council's decision. But the game was definitely called off. It would have been an interesting matchup and was not at all farfetched, only the timing of the year was not right. In fact, within less than a year a squad of collegians whose eligibility had just expired, Beattie Feathers being among them, would play a charity game in Chicago against the Bears. Red Cagle arrived in town on Tuesday afternoon and, finding out there was no game to be played, left that evening. A week later, Tennessee coach Bob Neyland was in Memphis attending an alumni banquet at the Peabody Hotel.

The Tigers remained together a few days longer, and when Henry Kelly, brother of Chicks' pitcher Harry Kelly, suffered a bad accident at a sawmill in Arkansas (a log fell on him while he was unloading a truck), they offered blood donations at the Baptist Hospital. A trip was scheduled to North Carolina to play the Bantams on Christmas Day, but it was canceled upon finding out that the Bantams had disbanded. It now seemed that the Tigers owed their existence more to habit than anything else. Several of them organized into a basketball team, and the football season concluded.

Nineteen thirty-three was a bust for the Tigers. They did not even play a NFL team at the end of the season, a legacy from the small crowds drawn by the Boston Braves the year before. But there was still more professional football to come. There was even hope and expectancy. In 1934 Godman founded a league, involving several Memphis notables in the venture, and once again the city mildly responded.

The American Football League

N 1934 THE FOOTBALL season began with something new. On August 31, the defending NFL champion Chicago Bears played a collection of college all stars in the first Annual College All-Star game. Sponsored by The Chicago Tribune, all proceeds, of which there were quite a lot, went to charity. Eighty thousand people packed into Soldier Field, far more than the 26,000 at Wrigley Field the previous December to witness the first official NFL Championship Game that pitted the Bears against the New York Giants, which the Bears won 23-21. Famous collegians pitted against pros aroused much curiosity, but the game itself was described as "deadly dull" and ended in a scoreless tie.

Earlier in the month Godman had issued a call for the organizational meeting of the new American Football League. He considered holding it in Chicago because of the All-Star game. "Our club owners can meet with National League officials and benefit a lot through their experience," he said. But the majority of club owners wanted it in Memphis where the league would be headquartered, and on Tuesday August 28 representatives from seven cities met in a conference room at the Chisca Hotel.

Wasting no time, the proceedings began with the men gathering behind a small, round table to work and have their picture taken: Tom Watkins, president of the Memphis Chicks and now committed to the Tigers, sat smiling in a vest and suit in the middle of the front row, behind him stood S. A. Godman, league president, and Bucky Moore, coach of the Louisville Bourbons.

Coaches Go Over Pro Situation With Officials

Coaches, officials' and magnates had numerous conferences here yesterday during the American League pro football meeting. Front, left to right, Tom Scott of Dallas, Tom Watkins, Memphis, and Sol Tenner, Charlotte, N. C. Back, S. A. Godman, league president, Bucky Moore, Louisville coach and Frosty Peters, Memphis coach.

American League officials and coaches

The meeting lasted only two days. Money matters were thrashed out, and a schedule was drawn up. Enthusiasm and harmony prevailed, and when it ended there was plenty of time to attend the All-Star game, which most of the men did, Godman, Watkins, and Frosty Peters leaving on Thursday night.

"As members of an accredited league," Godman told the press, "the teams will be able to secure the best players available. In the past, Southern teams have been handicapped by haphazard schedules during the early part of the season. This situation will be eliminated. The league will also promote rivalry between natural rival cities.

The American Football League was not the first professional football league of that name. Cash 'n' Carry Pyle had founded one in the midtwenties upon the drawing power of Red Grange, whom he had pirated away from the Bears, and it folded within a year. But unlike the league of Cash 'n' Carry Pyle, Godman's American League was not competing against the NFL and, therefore, posed no threat. In fact, the NFL hierarchy, club owners who had the most at stake, wisely saw it as an opportunity for growth in the professional game, something by which they would benefit. In Chicago, Jim McMillan, vice-president of the

Chicago Bears, called it, "The greatest thing that could happen to pro football in Dixie. I look for it to be a sure fire success."

The season would last from October 7 to December 8, and the league had six teams. It looked like there might be eight, but Houston, which was represented at the organizational meeting, never came through, and Jacksonville, Florida, another place of interest, was too far away. One team that could have entered, but chose not to, was the St. Louis Gunners, who still had their sights set on the NFL. (This caused repercussions later in the season when the St. Louis Blues, the best team in the new league, was forced to move to Kansas City.) Other cities in the league were Louisville, Charlotte, Tulsa, and Dallas, and good players were spread throughout.

Ram Coach

VIC SAUFLEY

Vic Saufley, one of the organizers and coach of the Dallas Rams, played end for the Memphis Tigers last year and he was a good one.

Vic Saufley

Bucky Moore, who was at the meeting, coached and played for the Louisville Bourbons, and the St. Louis Blues had a great halfback named George Grosvenor. The Tulsa Oilers had Billy Evans, an incredibly strong lineman, and Tony Holm coached and played for the Charlotte Puroils. So pervasive was the Tigers' influence (Vic Saufley was the coach of the Dallas Rams), that only two teams, Tulsa and St. Louis, did not have former Tigers at their helm when the season began.

The Tigers, at last playing every week against competitive peers, had a good team whose strength was mostly in the line. Cliff Norvell, developing over the years into one of the better linemen in professional football, and Danny Mc-Mullen were joined by some very good rookies and NFL veterans. Jess Eberdt had moved to Little Rock to work for a cement company, and replacing him at center was Art Koeninger (6' 3", 205 pounds) from the Philadelphia Eagles. Later in the season the Packers sent

Ex-Mississippians Starring for Tigers

COWBOY WOODRUFF
Back

BOB HERRINGTON
Back

These two Memphis Tiger backs played with Mississippi State, and fo, the Memphis pros, and are ex-are former stars with Mississippi Woodruff with Ole Miss. Both of pected to star in next Sunday's game State and Ole Miss. Herrington them have been playing fine football at Charlotte against the Bantams.

Woodruff and Herrington

down a tackle named Champ Seibold (6' 4", 235 pounds), and he would be the greatest Tiger lineman ever. The backfield was loaded with fast, shifty runners, but no one to dominate like Bucky Moore.

All their home games were played at Russwood Park, home of the Memphis Chicks, which was a larger stadium on Madison Avenue a few blocks west of Hodges Field, the grandstand providing 3,000 sheltered seats. They started practicing on Monday September 10 and moved into Russwood Park a week later, where equipment was distributed. The new uniforms were gold with black shoulders and black numbers.

Saussele and Cowboy Woodruff returned, but Maxwell thought they might get a back even better. "The Tigers [have] the inside track on Beattie Feathers if he doesn't make the grade with the Chicago Bears," he wrote in *The Commercial Appeal.* However, Feathers would be sensational in the NFL, and the Tigers instead signed Bobby "Runt" Herrington, a small left-handed quarterback from Mississippi State who the year before had been one of the Southeastern Conference's most outstanding players.

On Sunday morning, September 30, Maxwell wrote, "The Tigers appear considerably stronger than at any time the past two years. They are not experienced at certain spots but on the other hand, possess more versatility and are equipped with superior reserve forces." That afternoon they scrimmaged among themselves for three hours while several hundred fans watched. But before any of the players stepped out on the field, a meeting was held in the offices of Russwood Park, and the team was incorporated. Tom Watkins was elected president, and on the board were such prominent Memphians as Judge John D. Martin, and businessmen Bill Condon, William Loeb, Ed Koller, and Whitfield King. Peters appeared before them with detailed plans. There would be five home games. The season would open the next week in Dallas against the Dallas Rams, the game to be a feature of the Texas State Fair.

On its inaugural day Maxwell wrote that the American Football League "should be a success. The teams will be doing well to break even financially their first year. But, like the National League, things should be more prosperous year after year. I believe Louisville has the best club, with Memphis second and Charlotte third." On opening day Louisville defeated Charlotte 7-0, and the game that was to have been played in St. Louis between the Blues and the Oilers was postponed because of the World Series. (Dizzy and Daffy Dean were pitching the Cardinals to an insurmountable lead over the Detroit Tigers.)

Tigers vs Bourbons

In Dallas the Tigers won a close one 14-13. The first half was scoreless, but in the second half Memphis was unstoppable and scored on two long drives. But the Rams stayed in it with a ninety-seven-yard interception return by Red Tobin and then scored again in the final moments with a long pass only to miss the extra point. On the following week the Tigers played the Louisville Bourbons at Russwood in a game that became one of the most memorable social events of the year, because Mr. Watkins invited all seventeen of the season's most prominent debutantes. And in the South of the 1930s, debutantes were true celebrities. An honor based on wealth and social standing, their movements from luncheons to formal dinners were detailed in long newspaper articles throughout the fall and winter months.

The weather was warm during the week, and the Tigers practiced twice a day. It was still warm at the game on Sunday, though one of the debutantes was seen strolling before the

Coach Frosty Peters

stands with a red fox stole across her shoulders. Prior to the kickoff a band paraded up and down the field playing popular fight songs. Everett Cook, a World War I air ace and prominent cotton merchant, was seen aiming peanuts at a friend a few rows down as Sara and Blanche Crump, the young twin cousins of E. H. Crump, sat talking to their dates. City Hall had their own special section of the grandstand that was reserved for them by Commissioner Cliff Davis. Then the players trotted out on the field and the game got started.

The Tigers scored first after recovering a fumble and drove down the field for a field goal, and for a while they held off the Bourbons by keying on Moore and with Peters's long punts. But the Bourbons' huge line gradually wore them down as Louisville mounted long drives, opening up holes that their backs darted through. Twice the Tigers stopped them near the goal line, but in the third quarter the Bourbons finally broke loose. Moore completed a pass to Cavosi, and Cavosi galloped thirty yards for a touchdown. The Tigers resorted to long, desperate passes in the final minutes, which Louisville intercepted, and they lost by a score of 3-6.

"Four-thousand Memphians can't be wrong!" wrote Pigue the next day as if there had been no defeat. He continued:

THEY HAD THEIR first 1934 taste of professional football Sunday and found it good. The Tigers acquitted themselves well, altho appearing lacking in coordination, especially in their passing attack. [But] the kinks will be ironed out. All in all it was a happy day for the Memphians backing the professional grid sport for they were shown that Memphis football lovers are going to turn out to see the Tigers play.

The players did not take the defeat so lightly, and when they left for Charlotte on the following Saturday to play the Puroils, who were coming off a 0-21 trouncing by the Blues, they took along several large jugs of Memphis water, because it was believed that the year before the water in Charlotte had been the cause of several players becoming ill. The Puroils had gotten off to a poor start because of late preparation. Tony Holm had been hired as coach only two weeks before the season started, but

To Play Here Sunday

BUCKY MOORE
Halfback-Coach

JOHN NAG CAVOSI
Halfback

These two Louisville Bourbon footballers will be here Sunday to meet the Memphis Tigers at Russwood Park in the opener of the pigskin season in Memphis. Bucky is well known here, having played with the Tigers in years gone by. Cavosi is a tough hombre, and is expected to give the Tigers a lot of trouble stopping him.

Bourbons Moore and Cavosi

there was plenty of talent on their roster, and when the game started they played well against the Tigers.

Players went down with injuries on both sides, and reserves came off the bench. Dallas Long was the starting fullback for the Tigers, because Cowboy Woodruff had been kicked in the head against the Bourbons and was not yet fully recovered. But when

Jack Dempsey with Early Maxwell

the Puroils took the lead on a forty-five-yard pass, Woodruff was inserted and, capping a log drive in the third quarter, made a one-foot plunge into the end zone. However, the Tigers missed the extra point and were still trailing. Then, deep in their own territory in the waning minutes, a razzle-dazzle play by Peters, who took the snap from center and passed to end Burle Robinson, who lateraled to Cavette, who lateraled to Herrington, who ran down to the Charlotte 31-yard line, got them close enough for a field goal to win 9-7. Tony Holm was subsequently fired and replaced by a former all-Southern back from Georgia named Buster Mott, and the Puroils began playing better.

The Tigers, just as they had the year before, returned home from North Carolina riddled with injuries to face their toughest opponent of the year; this year the St. Louis Blues, who had just steamrolled previously unbeaten Louisville by making twenty-one first downs to the Bourbons' two, which prompted Bucky Moore to call them "the toughest pro 11 I've ever played against."

On Tuesday the Tigers shared Russwood Park with the Dallas Rams, who were traveling through Memphis on their way to Charlotte. Also in town were Ralph Depalma and Jack Dempsey. Depalma, winner of the Indianapolis 500, was just passing through, but Dempsey was refereeing wrestling matches at Ellis

Tiger Back and Lineman Plow Together

Reversing proceedings, Cliff Norvell, a guard, running under the protecting wing of Cowboy Woodruff, back. They'll both be running for the Memphis Tigers against Louisville in an American League game at Russwood Park. Staff Photo by Brubey

Norvell and Woodruff play together

Auditorium and was always surrounded by a retinue. "Dempsey is too good a fellow to shoo the sycophants away," wrote Pigue. "But he admitted that it was pretty tough at times, that they got in his hair, but that he could do nothing about it."

Some of the gloom caused by injuries was offset by the arrival of Erskine Walker, who as a fullback at Alabama had been one of the most feared running backs in the old Southern Conference. And on Thursday in an emotional meeting at Russwood Park, Woodruff and Joe Lilles, both still limping, implored Peters to take them to St. Louis. The players were ready to "throw the works" at the Blues, and if they could stop Grosvenor, who had rushed for 175 yards against Louisville, then victory, they thought, might be theirs. They boarded the train to St. Louis on

Saturday morning, October 27, and played on Sunday before 10,000 people.

The Blues started out strong, ripping through the Tigers' defense and advancing down the field for a touchdown. But the Tigers fought back, and the strength of their line began to prevail. There was no scoring in the second and third quarters, and in the fourth quarter fights broke out. Ellis Bashara of the Tigers, a professional wrestler in the off season, punched an opposing player and was ejected from the game. Then in the waning minutes Blues tackle Hugh Rhea lost his temper and punched Norvell. The Tigers had the ball at midfield, and their passing attack began to click. The penalty moved the ball to the St. Louis 27-yard line, where Herrington threw to Massad for fourteen yards and then to Robinson for a touchdown. The score was tied at 7-7 when, with the pop of a gun, the game ended.

Tom Watkins was elated. "It was great, great! The Tigers put on one of the best exhibitions of courage and football playing I have ever seen," he said. But Godman was concerned about the fights and pondered his authority as chairman of the new league. There had been a murder in Memphis on Saturday night, and it happened on the sidewalk outside the Chisca Hotel. Jim Clinkstock, a drunken sometimes-professional wrestler, killed a furniture dealer named Leon Kahn by beating and knocking

Walker and Champ Seibold

him to the pavement. No doubt, the violence of this incident happening just outside his office affected Godman, as he felt he could not condone it on the football field, and he fined Bashara and Rhea $25 each.

The Dallas Rams, losing to the Puroils 6-14, returned to Memphis and again shared Russwood Park with the Tigers. Their next game was against each other, and many people looked on as practices became competitive. The Rams rehearsed complicated plays with smooth precision. When the Tigers took the field, not to be outdone, they shot the ball around like it was a basketball, executing a double lateral to a forward pass followed by another lateral.

It was at this time that the Packers sent down Champ Seibold with the right to recall him the next year. In response, the Rams' owner, Miss Glyma Orr, the daughter of a rich Texan, caused a stir by sending Vic Sauffley to Chicago to sign some players from the NFL. When he returned on Friday with four players, Peters insisted that their contracts must be turned into league headquarters before they could be allowed to play. But on Sunday Glyma Orr, sitting among her players on the Dallas bench (which included the new members), was introduced to an applauding crowd by Mrs. Burr Chapman, the wife of a wealthy, local lumberman. And despite the competitive practices, the game itself was marred by errors. Bad laterals and inspired Rams defense within the shadows of their goal posts killed Tiger drives. In the second quarter Champ Seibold and Red Tobin of the Rams came to a harsh, belated recognition when Seibold, a former all-American at Wisconsin, smacked into Tobin, who had

Slim Coach, Hefty Kick

Frosty Peters who coaches the pro Tigers of Memphis can show his charges plenty in the way of kicking. He's demonstrating here.

Peters in fine form

Rival Backs in Sunday's Pro Game

RED TOBIN
Ex-Notre Dame Back, with Dallas

MIKE MASSAD
Ex-Oklahoma Back, with Tigers

Rival Backs

played at Notre Dame. They had played against each other in college, and Seibold's hit jarred Tobin's memory.

The Tigers took an early lead on a beautiful forty-six-yard field goal that soared and spiraled through the goal posts. But in the third quarter the Rams blocked a punt, and Tobin picked up the ball to dash down the sidelines for a touchdown. Then the Tigers blocked a punt, and the ball rolled into the end zone and out of bounds for a safety. Trailing 5-7 in the fourth quarter the Tigers moved close enough for Peters to kick another field goal and won 8-7.

"Cash customers stayed until the last play," wrote Pigue. "The Tigers are becoming more and more popular with Memphis pigskin fans, and it appears as if pro football has at last struck pay dirt in Memphis."

Glyma Orr's players saw her off at Union Station with the promise of a victory next Sunday in St. Louis. Red Tobin replaced Vic Sauffley as coach as they remained in Memphis until Wednesday, departing for Kansas City rather than St. Louis. The Gunners had at last made it to the NFL, and the Blues, not wanting to compete at the gate, moved to Kansas City. Ironically,

The Tulsa Game

the Blues had helped elevate the Gunners when on the previous Wednesday they defeated the Cincinnati Reds 35-0; a defeat as bad as any the Reds had suffered, and, having already lost seven straight games, they then folded, their NFL franchise purchased by the Gunners, their players distributed among many teams in both leagues. The Blues had solidified their hold on the league lead with a 21-7 trouncing of the Bourbons, leaving the Tigers one game behind in sole possession of second place with a record of 3-1-1.

"The Tiger line is conceded by every coach in the league as comparing favorably with any in the older National League and is by far the best in the American circuit," wrote Pigue. But they were handicapped on offense by the lack of a strong fullback. Woodruff was still injured, and Ernest Massad, the Syrian halfback who had terrorized them the year before as an Oklahoma Chief, was too light for the heavy duty he had been thrust into. Peters sent off wires to the NFL, and the Packers responded by sending down 210-pound Hank Ross, whom Seibold said was a powerful line plunger. There were five league games left to play. Attendance was up from the year before, and their next opponent was the winless Tulsa Oilers, who had just bolstered their squad with players from the defunct Cincinnati Reds.

Though everyone else in the league was able to beat the Oilers, to the Tigers they became a nemesis. Their first game against each other was played in perfect football weather, a windy, cool, clear November afternoon at Russwood Park, and the Oilers showed unexpected strength and speed and a crowd-pleasing, 240-pound tackle named Billy Evans.

Three thousand people attended the hard-fought game. It was an unlucky draw for the Tigers. They had acquired a great lineman only to have him pitted against one even better. Evans was short and barrel-chested with long arms and big hands and an uncanny knack for following the ball. He stalked runners and brought them down like a wild animal capturing prey. Yet his nature was genial. Seibold fought him brutally and eventually knocked him out, but never did he get his goat. Evans would rise after a fall, smile, and shake hands.

The Tigers scored first on a razzle-dazzle passing combination in the second quarter. A few minutes later the Oilers scored on a disputed play when an Oiler lineman emerged from a pileup with the ball tucked under his arm and lumbered thirty yards to the end zone. The Tigers protested that he had wrested the ball from Massad, but officials let the touchdown stand. Evans preserved the tie with a flying tackle of Massad in the second half. Finally, late in the fourth quarter, Seibold finally took the big tackle's measure as Evans staggered punch drunk to the sidelines. But the damage had been done. The final score was 6-6, and the two teams would play again in the heat of the Mississippi Delta on the following Friday night.

Not faring well at the box office, the Oilers had lost use of the stadium in Tulsa, the first noticeable crack in the new American League, so Watkins and other officials met with the Clarksdale Football Association and arranged to have the game played down there. This would be the first professional football game, not counting a few charity games between pickup teams, to be played in Mississippi. The Oilers made the trip by bus on Thursday, and the Tigers left on Friday. Something new was reported in the afternoon papers. Further south, down in New Orleans, 300 visionary men with $100 apiece planned on the New Year to stage the first annual Sugar Bowl to celebrate and honor the vast sugarcane fields of Louisiana.

The city of Memphis also had something new. What had been a dumping ground on eroding river bluffs, ghastly in

Riverside Drive

appearance, was now a smooth, paved highway gracefully running along sodded banks. Built by money obtained from the Public Works Administration, the new road was called Riverside Drive.

The game in Clarksdale was played in a small, lighted stadium, and the Oilers won it for their first and only victory of the season, the final score being 3-6. On the play that Tulsa scored the winning touchdown, Tiger back Massad, who had earlier kicked a field goal, remained on the ground afterward with a broken arm and was lost for the season. The Tigers always had trouble against teams from Oklahoma, and their record dropped to 3-2-2, virtually eliminating them from contention for the league title because in Kansas City the Blues continued to remain undefeated. But the Tigers regrouped and traveled to Louisville on the following weekend.

In the North, where professional football was seeing true growth, the Chicago Bears were a team for the ages. Damon Runyon wrote, "The Bears are called one of the greatest football teams in history. The great Bronko Nagurski, a player who ranks with the best backfield men who ever lived, is a bull of a man [and] takes out two or three men at a time." The beneficiary of Nagurski's blocking was Beattie Feathers, averaging better than nine yards per carry and shattering NFL rushing records. "Following this guy Nagurski is just like following a truck," said Feathers.

Plenty of Heft Behind This

Bronco Nagurski of the Bears has 230 pounds behind his short tosses, and he will probably hurl plenty of them against the Tigers at Russwood Sunday. Nagurski is one of the greatest of pro football players.

Bronco Nagurski

Runyon believed that college teams, such as "Minnesota, Princeton, Navy, Alabama, Temple or Colgate would have no chance with a pro team like the Bears. Eventually professional football franchises in the big city will be worth as much as baseball franchises."

The Tigers practiced well on Thursday and Friday, signed Red Tobin when he quit the Rams, and left for Louisville "in the pink" early Saturday morning. Now late November, Notre Dame defeated Army before 81,000 at Yankee Stadium, and on Sunday the Tigers stunned the Bourbons. In the first quarter Saussele returned a punt for a touchdown and Louisville, playing without Bucky Moore, could thereafter muster only a field goal. The Tigers, gaining consistently through the line, put the game out of reach in the fourth quarter when Tobin rushed into the end zone and won 17-3 to reclaim sole possession of second place.

The Tulsa Oilers returned to Memphis on their way back from Charlotte, where they had lost to the Puroils 0-25, and stayed overnight. "Our big men were stopped in their tracks," said their coach about the defeat. "All we could gain the entire afternoon was 35 yards." On Thursday afternoon they worked out at Russwood Park, their only reminder of what glory might have been, then boarded a bus back to Tulsa and, as it turned out, oblivion. They were disbanded by the end of the week, an ominous note for the new league's future, and forfeited their game against the Kansas City Blues.

When the much-improved Puroils arrived on Friday night, Buster Mott predicted that what had happened to the Oilers last Sunday would also happen to the Tigers in Memphis on Sunday. Fred Hambright, who before had been used as a blocking back, was now running with the football, and he proved to be power-ful and bruising. "I wouldn't let him go for less than $5000," bragged Mott. But the power plays that had worked so well for the Tigers in Louisville were still clicking in practice, and, since it was not yet known that the Blues would win by forfeit, there was still a chance for the championship.

Twenty-five hundred fans attended the game, and the de-fense rose to the occasion. Seibold and Norvell played very well, and the onrushing Tiger ends were deadly. Charlotte went scoreless, and in the fourth quarter Saussele broke loose. He wandered around right end for forty-seven yards, sidestepping and outrunning through a field dotted with Puroils, until fi-nally caught by Branch at the Charlotte 23, and after a se-ries of pile drives the ponderous Rose dove into the end zone. Then Saussele broke loose again, running from midfield to the 19-yard line where, hemmed in by tacklers, he lateraled to Buckley, who caught it on a bounce and went another twelve yards. (On this play George Maugin, the Puroil guard, suffered a ruptured kidney when clipped from behind and was taken to the Methodist Hospital where doctors had to operate.) Mott protested loudly, claiming that the lateral had been a forward pass. The fans razzed him, and he cussed the fans. The game threatened to break out in a flurry of fights, but officials let the play stand, and Peters kicked a field goal to make the final score 13-0.

The Blues had clinched the championship. The best the Ti-gers could do was finish in second place. Four players from Kansas City made the first team of the Associated Press all-star squad, picked by sportswriters in league cities. The Tigers placed two on the first team, Burle Robinson and Red Tobin, and Seibold, McMullen, Peters, and Woodruff made honorable mention. Later in the week when the *Memphis Press-Scimitar* came out with an all-star team, it put four Tigers on the first team: Seibold, McMullen, Saussele, and Robinson; four more on the second team, and named George Maugin, still in the hospital, a first-team guard. But both polls agreed that George Grosvenor was the league's most valuable player. Weighing only 175-pounds, Grosvenor would in the following years become a star in the NFL.

Pigue wrote,

BEATTIE FEATHERS HAS a real rival in George Grosvenor.
Grosvenor, also in his first pro year, has a better average gain
per game. The Blues quarterback has piled up a total of 868
yards in seven league games. In addition to that [he] has established himself as the best pass heaver in the American League,
completing throws for a total of 477 yards, giving him a grand
total of 1345 yards. Ted Saussele of Memphis is the nearest
threat to Grosvenor for yardage with 524, while Johnny Branch
of Charlotte trails him with passes, completing heaves for 215.

Grosvenor also did most of the Blues punting, averaging
39.5 yards. Peters was the only one better with a 40.3 average.

When the Blues and the Tigers played on Sunday December
9 it was the grand finale for the American League. During the
week Peters tried to resurrect the aerial attack in practice. The
Blues had allowed only two first downs and twenty-six points
scored against them. They arrived Saturday morning and worked
out at Russwood Park. Their backfield was definitely superior
with Grosvenor and Tony Kaska, "The Touchdown Twins," tied
for the league lead in points with fifty-four each. Peters told reporters, "We have to beat them and I believe the boys are ready
for the toughest game of the year."

The weather was cold and 3,000 fans, Bucky Moore with his
hometown bride among them, shivered in the stands. Congressman Crump rose to his feet several times during the game and
urged everybody to "stand up and help the Tigers to victory."
The Blues had a smooth, powerful attack as Grosvenor and
Kaska bucked, sidestepped, and passed down the field. In the
first quarter Kaska plunged into the end zone. The Tigers played
desperately to stay in the game, and tied the score in the second quarter when Walker intercepted and ran twenty-two yards
down the sidelines for a touchdown. But the Blues regained the
lead before the end of the half as Grosvenor rifled long passes
to Ashburn and Frahm, then went off tackle to score. It was
tied again in the third quarter when Walker caught a pass from
Tobin deep in Blues' territory and sped into the end zone. But
the Blues drove back down the field, and Kaska crashed across

Menace to Tiger Pros

Memphis' Tigers will have to keep their eyes on George Grosvenor, Kansas City triple threater, Sunday. Grosvenor leads the American League in ground gaining and passing and is tied for scoring honors.

George Grosvenor of the Blues

the goal line, his two touchdowns giving him the league scoring title, and the Blues won 21-14. They were clearly the better team. When Saussele ran with the ball, he lacked interference. Grosvenor had been artful, uncannily picking the precise spot to make his cuts and keeping the Tigers guessing by mixing runs with accurate passing. In the only other American League game on this day, Dallas defeated Charlotte 13-7.

It was much colder in New York City that afternoon, where at the Polo Grounds the undefeated Chicago Bears played the Giants for the NFL Championship. Overnight rain and freezing temperatures of –9 degrees had turned the field into a sheet of ice. Beattie Feathers, suffering a dislocated shoulder three weeks before, did not play, but Nagurski rushed for a touchdown and Jack Manders kicked a field goal as the Bears skated to a 10-3 half time lead.

During the half the Giants' coach, Steve Owen, dispatched an assistant to Manhattan College for basketball sneakers, which were then worn by some of the Giants when they trotted back onto the field. The difference was dramatic. In the third quarter Manders kicked another field goal to increase the Bears' lead. But, suddenly, the Giants stopped skidding, and the Bears kept sliding, and the Giants' great halfback Ken Strong, he who had once been a Tiger, began to run hard. They exploded for twenty-seven points in the fourth quarter, past the helpless, sliding Bears, and won 30-13 in an astonishing turnabout. Forty-one thousand fans went wild, hundreds stormed the field, and years later George Halas would still moan, "I often wonder whether it isn't better to be lucky than good."

In the final American League standings the Tigers finished third with a record of 5-2-2. Louisville (5-3) was second. Dallas (3-5), Charlotte (3-7), and Tulsa (1-7) made up the bottom half. Pigue commented on the closing of the season:

PROFESSIONAL FOOTBALL HAS not been the financial success that the backers had hoped it would be. Education of the fans was the big thing this year. This fall, despite a fine attraction all season, the Tigers did not emerge on the black side of the ledger. The Tigers will be back again next season, however, and believe they'll begin to cash in on their investment, for interest in pro football is getting keener season after season, and Memphis some day will be one of the pay-dirt spots for the pro pigskin sport.

The Tigers did return the following season, but not like before. Though not yet publicly known, the American Football League was finished, and with it the Tigers' demise was assured.

But the words written by Pigue, "Interest in pro football is getting keener season after season, and Memphis will some day be one of the pay-dirt spots . . .," now have a strong echo; not because it was a prediction, but because it was actively thought and put into print as long ago as 1934.

And for the Tigers the effort spent on the American League helped bring about a high season finale. They again ended against NFL teams. Their last game of the season would be against the great Chicago Bears. But before that, on December 18, they would host the Brooklyn Dodgers. Seibold had left the squad, Tobin and Walker were persuaded to stay on, and the backfield was bolstered by a former all-Southern half back from Tulane named Floyd "Little Preacher" Roberts.

Ex-Army Star Coming

CHRIS CAGLE

This former Army grid star will ship Tigers next Sunday at Russwood Park. Cagle is rated as one of the greatest ball carriers in the lineup of the Brooklyn Dodgers when they meet the Memphis game.

Six All-Americans In Dodgers' Lineup Sunday

Cagle, Montgomery, Grossman, Hickman And Others to Collide With Tigers

Chris Cagle of the Dodgers

The Dodgers had finished third in the eastern conference of the NFL with a record of 4-7. At the beginning of the season Chris Cagle sold his share of the team to Dan Topping, the future owner of baseball's New York Yankees, and their fine quarterback Benny Friedman retired to coach at the college level. With Friedman gone so went their aerial attack, but Herman Hickman's blocking kept the offense from complete moribundity as Cagle, Ralph Kerchival, and Shipwreck Kelly (a part-owner) gained yards despite being the victims of keying defenses. A small group of players lead by Stumpy Thomason reached Memphis on Monday, and Thomason was interviewed by Pigue saying,

> THE GIANTS WERE lucky to beat the Bears. The Bears really have a great football club, and they missed Beattie Feathers in

there Sunday. He's a great football player and the hardest man to tackle I ever saw. It's true he had wonderful interference from Nagurski and the other great Bear blockers, but Feathers would stand out on any team.

And he thought Steve Owens had outsmarted Halas. "It was the first time, to my knowledge, that rubber basketball shoes have ever been used in a football game, but it worked. I believe the Bears could beat the Giants four out of five games with plenty of room to spare."

On Saturday night at the Orpheum a newsreel of the championship game was shown featuring Ken Strong in several sensational runs. The next day the Tigers took the field against the biggest team they had ever faced. The Dodgers line averaged 226 pounds (the Tigers averaged 212 pounds), and they came out wearing gold pants and dark jerseys. It was cool, the sky was partly cloudy, and several prominent politicians, the mayor, congressman Crump, and the governor of Tennessee, were in the crowd.

The Dodgers scored quickly on a thirty-yard pass from Kelly, a tall almost gangling back, to Wayland Becker and threatened

Six Hefty Dodgers Ready for a Row With Tigers

Six sturdy Brooklyn Dodgers who will tear at the Tigers in the professional game at Russwood Park this afternoon. From left to right: Becker, Matson, Worden, Sanson, Thomason and Kelly.

Brooklyn Dodgers Line

to run away with it. They dominated the line of scrimmage, pushing the Tigers all over the field, as Kelly reeled off long gains around the ends and accurately flipped passes to teammates. But Saussele had a good day; breaking loose once, he might have gone all the way had not Thomason pushed him out of bounds. And the Tigers actually outrushed the Dodgers, but whenever they approached the goal line the Brooklyn defense stiffened.

Early in the fourth quarter Kelly intercepted and galloped fifty yards down the right sideline, outrunning three Tigers and eluding another, and gamboled into the end zone. Now down by fourteen points, the Tigers made a game of it by reaching the Brooklyn 18-yard line with help from a pass interference call, and a razzle-dazzle play to follow-up with Peters going off tackle and lateraling to Norvell, who ran for the touchdown to make the score 7-14. Then they got the ball back and drove downfield again, but Becker intercepted and swept through a broken field for another Brooklyn touchdown to make the final score 7-20. On this same day in St. Louis the Kansas City Blues fared no better; defeated by the Gunners, who were about to lose their NFL franchise and fade into obscurity, 0-7 before 7,500 people.

The Bears were even bigger than the Dodgers, and, remembering back to 1929 when Saunders had stacked his roster with NFL stars, Halas demanded that the Tigers could add only one NFL player. However, once made, the agreement was immediately broken with the signing of 226-pound tackle Milo Lubratovich and end Harry Kloppenberg from the Dodgers, and it was ignored later in the week, much to Halas's approval, when two New York Giants were also signed.

The Tigers needed all the help they could get. The Chicago Bears, comparable in size to modern pro teams, were the greatest football team up to that time. Their line was the most powerful ever assembled; spearheaded at center by Eddie Kawal (6' 2", 205 pounds) with Walt Keisling (6' 3", 246 pounds) and Joe Kopcha (6', 226 pounds) at guards, the aging but still very strong Link Lyman (6' 2", 246 pounds) and young George Musso (6' 2", 268 pounds) were the tackles, with Bill Hewitt and Luke Johnsos, backed by the able Bill Karr, at ends. In the backfield were Bronko Nagurksi (6' 2", 230 pounds) and Beattie Feathers in his record-breaking rookie year. (Feathers had rushed for 1,052 yards—a record that would not be broken for thirteen seasons.) Gene Ronzani (5' 9", 200 pounds) and Bernie Masterson (6' 3", 195 pounds) took turns directing a very effective passing attack, and "Automatic" Jack Manders did the kicking. Manders, by kicking ten field goals and earning a reputation as pro football's first great place kicker, had brought new heights to that part of the game. Red Grange, playing in his last season, had been reduced to a reserve.

The Bears were also successful at the gate, clearing more than $100,000 in profit, and paid their players an average salary of $5,000. Nagurski was the highest-paid player, followed by Grange, whose best income came from outside interests such as radio, movies, and the stage. Pitiful by comparison, the Tigers had lost $7,000, and their average weekly payroll was about $900.

The price of a ticket rose to $2.20, but advance sales were good. "It will be worth every penny to see such great stars as Nagurski, Beattie Feathers, Jack Manders and others," wrote Pigue. And the attraction was increased when Mel Hein and Dale Burnett, two celebrated New York Giants passing through town on their way to the West Coast, agreed to stay over through Sunday's game. Both men practiced with the Tigers on Wednesday, and, realizing that a stronger Tiger roster meant a larger gate, Halas okayed their signing. Grange called Burnett, whose hometown was Earle, Arkansas, the best pass receiver in the NFL. He and Hein spoke over the radio. "We've played against the Bears three times and I like the idea of meeting them again," Burnett said.

And Hein, "Sure Feathers is good, but in both games he played against the Giants we managed to bottle him up. Nagurski is a terror if you allow him to get a good running start, but

Make Way for Manders

Jack Manders

A Couple of New York Behemoths Don Uniforms of Tigers

Those Memphis Tigers picked up some real power when Mel Hein and Dale Burnett of the New York Giants showed up at Russwood yesterday. Hein is over the ball, with Walker, Coach Peters and Nisonger looking on, while Burnett gets set for the one-handed pass

New Tiger Signees

he can be stopped by one man if you hit him from the side or tackle him below his knees. Otherwise I doubt one man can stop him." Mel Hein, a 225-pound center-linebacker and one of the first men inducted into the Hall of Fame, knew of what he spoke. His confrontations with Nagurski were that era's equivalent of Jim Brown versus Sam Huff. He was staying with his wife at the Devoy Hotel downtown on the corner of Front and Jefferson.

Amidst rumors that Feathers might not be playing, a phone call was made to Chicago, where Halas replied, "Feathers is the star Memphis fans want most to see. We've given his shoulder ample time to heal and the club physician says he's okay now." And he wired down the names of twenty-two players he was bringing along. But first the Bears traveled to Knoxville, where on Saturday in ankle-deep mud at a baseball park (denied use of Shield-Watkins Field because of the University of Tennessee's "opposition to professional football," *The Commercial Appeal* retorted this incident by writing, "The next five years will see a pro team in every American city of 250,000 or more.") they defeated the Brooklyn Dodgers 20-7, then crossed the state and arrived in Memphis in the early-morning hours, spending the rest of the night at the Devoy Hotel. It had been raining since Wednesday, but on Sunday, two days before Christmas, the sky cleared, the sun warmed, and the Bears played like Rose Bowl contenders.

The Elks band struck up with football tunes as fans filed into the stadium. Down on the field as the teams warmed up, Dale Burnett stood out, easily distinguished by a large, white bandage covering a wound on his chin. The Bears kicked off at 2:15. The Tigers received; their drive stalled. Burnett punted to midfield, and the Bears wasted no time scoring. Manders ripped through the line for fifteen yards, then Masterson dropped back and tossed a neat spiral to Molesworth, and Molesworth scampered into the end zone. When they got the ball back a few minutes later, Manders kicked a long field goal. The Bears' blocking was precise, they tackled fiercely, seldom leaving an opening, and moved the ball at will.

Beattie Feathers of the Bears in a characteristic heaving pose as he passes one to Bill Karr, snagging end.

Beattie Feathers of the Bears

Feathers came off the bench in the second quarter, heavily taped with much padding around his right shoulder, and brought the crowd to its feet with a twisting and turning thirty-five-yard run. Then Nagurski got the ball and thundered around right end for thirteen yards, carrying tacklers along with him, to set up another touchdown. The game looked like a rout, but suddenly, near the end of the first half, the Tigers came alive. Saussele returned a punt fifty yards to the Bears' 37-yard line, and on the next play Tobin dropped back, was almost caught, and scrambled toward the sideline where he was almost caught again. Bottled up, he spotted Saussele and hurled the ball downfield. Saussele caught it on the run and ran into the end zone. The Elks band struck up, and at halftime the score was 7-17.

Halas staged an incident in the third quarter when he rushed onto the field and yelled at officials after a Bear touchdown had been called back. If the fans came to see the Poppa Bear, he gave them a good look, and, making the most of the opportunity, they razzed him and threw down bags of peanuts. Halas was undaunted, relishing the situation he had created, and strolled back to the bench casually picking up the hurled nuts and popping them into his mouth. Then he was overheard telling his players to give "the works," and the Bears went down the field on another scoring binge.

Masterson threw a touchdown to Johnsos, and Feathers came off the bench again to carry twice for long yardage and set up a plunge by Manders. As the final seconds ticked off the clock, the Tigers scored once more. Burnett heaved long passes to Robinson and then hit Reasor for a touchdown, and the game ended 13-30. Sadly, Red Grange had spent the entire afternoon sitting on the bench with a sock covering his broken toe.

Though it had ended with a defeat and the Tigers' record dropped to 5-5-2, the season finished on a high note with the visit by the Bears. Three thousand five hundred and twenty-three people, an accurate count, had paid their way into the game, and the Elks Fund realized $1,265.92. The team disbanded, and the players went home for the holidays. Professional football in an earlier era was just about over in Memphis.

THE END OF AN ERA

THE AMERICAN FOOTBALL LEAGUE lost $50,000 in the first and what would be its only year of operation, a huge amount in The Depression. Still, in the summer of 1935 a meeting was held in the Chisca Hotel to try and organize for another season. A promoter from California named B. B. Nelson, wanting a team in Los Angeles, agreed to guarantee expenses for sending teams out to play on the West Coast, but this was an idea ahead of its time. However, several Southern cities were considering teams if Memphis would have an entry. But investors from last year's team had disappeared. Tom Watkins coyly told Godman and James Mathews that he would put up a sum if others could be found to match it.

Attempting to revive a dying situation, a death he might have felt could somewhat diminish professional football, or at least temporarily inhibit the progress of its growth, Halas expressed interest in having the Tigers become a farm team for the Bears. On September 6 *The Commercial Appeal* reported, "Halas believes in the future of the sport in Dixie and thinks it won't be long until the American League will be ready to meet the National in a pro grid World Series." But actually the future of the Tigers and the American Football League looked very dim. Godman and Mathews tried vainly to line up investors. Mathews, a man not easily discouraged, at last admitted, "It looks pretty bleak." The league officially folded in late September, its last meeting held in Columbus, Ohio. But the Tigers still played a few more games.

Cavette and Norvell mustered together another team and secured the use of Hodges Field. Cavette told the press, "We will limit our squad to 16 or 17 men and they will all have to play tough and fighting football, even rough football at times, to stick." And he urged interested men with college or even prep experience to try out. Any profit would be shared by the players. Koeninger, Buckley, and Herrington were back, and from previous years there were Joe Gee, Seiberling, and Blankenbaker. They opened the season on Sunday October 27 against a pick-up team called the Helena Seaporters who had "Little Preacher" Roberts and Johnny Faulkner on their roster.

The sky was dark and threatening, again the weather was jinxed, and though admission was only 55¢, less than 700 people showed up. Dick Dorsey, a rookie halfback from Tennessee, broke through the center of the line and outran Roberts for a touchdown in the first quarter. Then there came a downpour of rain, and the rest of the scores came on miscues. The Tigers won 13-6; Norvell had recovered a fumble that set up the short drive to give them victory.

Roberts and Faulkner were signed, and on the following Sunday the Tigers smashed the West Tennessee All-Stars 52-0 at Hodges Field. Barely mentioned in the papers anymore, it was their last home game, and the city was hardly aware. They had one more game to play, and that would be on the road.

It was Saturday November 9. Sunny streets were littered with dead, brown leaves, and as Ole Miss and Tennessee played for the first time in Memphis, the stands at new Crump Stadium were packed with over 30,000 people. On this day the Tigers were traveling to Greenwood, Mississippi, where the next day they played before a small but enthusiastic crowd at Legion Field. Their opponent, fittingly enough, was the Hominey Indians, whom they dominated this last time, scoring twenty-one points in the first quarter on their way to a 34-0 victory.

Then they left the field for good, even though they still tried to schedule more games. It seemed certain that the St. Louis Gunners, also having a bleak fall, were coming to Memphis on the first of December. And the Tigers continued practicing and announced a starting lineup. But when the time arrived for the game to take place, the Gunners had disbanded. Oh, how obscure it had all become, and, still, there was talk of another game. Several former Tennessee players had supposedly banded together and were seeking a game with the Tigers, and that was the last that anyone heard.

The city could not have had a better football team, at least not on the field. The Tigers accumulated a record of 52-22-9 and never had a losing season. Anything better, by now, would have taken on mythical proportions. They organized and took to the field against long odds and played against and sometimes beat the best teams in the country. And they did leave a permanent legacy: in honor of a winning tradition, the athletic teams at the University of Memphis took their name from the Tigers; this done by Zack Curlin, the former referee who became the school's athletic director in the early 30s.

Oh, come back Clarence Saunders, Bettencourt, Applewhite, and Bucky Moore. Come back Ernie Nevers, Early Maxwell, Peters, and Monk Godman. Such effort is never wasted; in part, it's why we live. Your legions, ghostly now, had a true, eternal spirit. Come back, come back, and take the field again.

BIBLIOGRAPHY

George Treadwell (President, Memphis Professional Football Association, 1930, 1932), in discussion with the author, March 1985.

Harkins, John. *Metropolis of the American Nile*. Oxford, Mississippi: The Guild Bindery Press, 1982.

Neft, David S., Roland Johnson, Richard M. Cohen, and Jordan A. Deutsch. *The Sports Encyclopedia: Pro Football*. New York: Grosset & Dunlap, 1974.

Red Cavette (former player for the Memphis professional football Tigers, 1927 – 1935), in discussion with the author, April 1987.

Reid, Panthea. "William Faulkner's "War Wound": Reflections on Writing and Doing, Knowing and Remembering." *The Virginia Quarterly Review* 74 (Autumn 1998): http://www.vqronline.org/essay/william-faulkner's-war-wound-reflections-writing-and-doing-knowing-and-remembering.

Whittingham, Richard. *The Chicago Bears*. New York: Simon & Schuster, 1986.

Sources: Almost all of the information that I used to write *Tigers by the River* was derived from the two main Memphis newspapers of the era, *The Commercial Appeal* and the *Memphis Press-Scimitar*. *The Commercial Appeal* was the morning newspaper; the *Memphis Press-Scimitar* appeared in the afternoon. There were no books or articles available on the subject of the Memphis professional football Tigers. The Memphis/Shelby County Archivist could only find a single article from a more recent newspaper about Zach Curlin naming the local college sports teams after Clarence Saunders's Sole Owner Tigers. Of course, I wanted more, and so at the direction of the staff of the main library on Peabody I started combing through microfilm of the old newspapers. Articles about the team began appearing in the sports sections of both newspapers in October 1927 and continued through November 1935 when the team fell out of existence. I started researching the story in the winter of 1985 and finished the research about three years later. Along the way I gleaned much information about the city and its people at this time; much of which, though very interesting, I could not use as part of the story. The brief biography of Clarence Saunders, who was a very prominent man at the time of the story, was gathered from articles in both newspapers written about him by editors and staff writers during the years covered. I limited my research to the falls and early winters of each year. The articles I read were too numerous to list, approaching nearly a thousand, but the four principal writers were Early Maxwell, first as reporter with *The Commercial Appeal*, later with the *Memphis Press-Scimitar*; Naylor Stone of the *Memphis Press-Scimitar*; Walter Stewart, sports editor of the *Memphis Press-Scimitar*; and Bob Pigue, also of the *Memphis Press-Scimitar*.

ABOUT THE AUTHOR

WYLIE MCLALLEN grew up in Memphis, Tennessee, where his family has deep historical roots. At the University of Tennessee he obtained a degree in History and English and, under a distinguished man of Southern Letters, Professor Robert Drake, studied Fiction and Composition: Dr. Drake was able to personally introduce his students to the poet and novelist James Dickey, and was a close friend of author Flannery O'Conner. Wylie worked as a programmer analyst at Malone & Hyde Inc. in Memphis and later owned a small business services center. He currently resides with his wife, Nickey Bayne, in Vancouver, British Columbia, where they have raised two now grown children. He continues to write both history and fiction.

CPSIA information can be obtained
at www.ICGtesting.com
Printed in the USA
LVOW12s2002050717
540364LV00001B/80/P